TL;DR

The **On Campus** imprint of UBC Press features publications designed for the diverse members of the university community – students, faculty, instructors, staff, and administrators.

On Campus offers a range of interesting, sometimes unconventional, but always useful information. All **On Campus** works are assessed by experts in the field prior to publication. To ensure affordability, PDFs are available as free downloads from the UBC Press website, with print and other digital formats also available through our website, bookstores, and libraries.

On Campus books are designed to help readers successfully meet the intellectual and social challenges encountered at university or college today and include:

How to Succeed at University (and Get a Great Job!):
Mastering the Critical Skills You Need for School, Work, and Life,
by Thomas R. Klassen and John A. Dwyer
(also available in French from University of Ottawa Press)

It's All Good (Unless It's Not): Mental Health Tips and Self-Care
Strategies for Your Undergrad Years, by Nicole Malette

You @ the U: A Guided Tour through Your First Year of University,
by Janet Miller

The Successful TA: A Practical Approach to Effective Teaching,
by Kathy M. Nomme and Carol Pollock

To find out more about **On Campus** books visit www.ubcpress.ca.

TL;DR

A Very Brief Guide to Reading and Writing in University

Joel Heng Hartse

32 31 30 29 28 27 26 25 24 23   5 4 3 2 1

Printed in Canada on FSC-certified ancient-forest-free paper
(100% post-consumer recycled) that is processed chlorine- and acid-free.

Library and Archives Canada Cataloguing in Publication

Title: TL;DR : a very brief guide to reading and writing in university /
Joel Heng Hartse.
Other titles: Too long; didn't read
Names: Hartse, Joel Heng, author.
Description: Includes bibliographical references.
Identifiers: Canadiana (print) 20230229522 | Canadiana (ebook) 20230229557
ISBN 9780774839143 (softcover) | ISBN 9780774839150 (PDF)
ISBN 9780774839167 (EPUB)
Subjects: LCSH: Academic writing. | LCSH: English language—Rhetoric.
Classification: LCC LB2369 .H37 2023 | DDC 808.02—dc23

UBC Press gratefully acknowledges the financial support for our publishing
program of the Government of Canada (through the Canada Book Fund),
the Canada Council for the Arts, and the British Columbia Arts Council.

Printed and bound in Canada by Friesens
Set in Acumin Variable and Source Sans Pro by Gerilee McBride
Copy editor: Lesley Erickson
Cover designer: Gerilee McBride

UBC Press
The University of British Columbia
2029 West Mall
Vancouver, BC V6T 1Z2

www.ubcpress.ca

This is for Ollie and Ben; may your nascent
love of reading and other forms of making meaning
bring you joy for the rest of your lives.

Contents

A Note for Students

You don't have to read this book all the way through. You can just dip in and out of it as needed.

In fact, if you don't have time to read the rest of this book, just read this list.

How to Get Better at Writing

1 Recognize it will take a long time.

2 Read a lot.

3 Write a lot.

4 Have lots of other people read your writing and give you feedback.

5 Be aware that no one person's ideas about writing will be exactly right for your particular context.

6 Don't leave all the work to the last minute.

7 Use whatever method of proofreading works for you, but definitely use one.

8 Know your audience and their expectations by asking questions and doing your own research (see no. 2).

9 Multitasking doesn't work. Don't do ten other things on your computer or phone while you're writing.

10 Unless advised otherwise, never use any font but twelve-point Times New Roman (double-spaced) for the rest of your life. It will just make everything a lot simpler.

A Note for Instructors

I wrote this during the period when we all had to switch to online instruction due to the COVID pandemic (remember that?), and I didn't want to force my students to buy a textbook, because some of them couldn't even leave their home countries, let alone make a trip to our university's bookstore. I tried to strip my writing class down to its bare essentials, but I found there were still things I wanted to explain to students in ways that didn't work very well over a Zoom lecture.

So I set out to write the world's shortest writing textbook. My goal was to write in a direct, no BS, friendly, informal way and to be honest about what I see as important for succeeding in first-year writing courses and the early stages of undergraduate programs generally. Not everyone will agree with me, and doubtless what I think of as "important" is shaped by my own experiences. (For example, my doctoral training was in applied linguistics, and I do not work in an English department, which may be quite different from the backgrounds of many people who teach first-year writing.)

I can envision this book being used in several ways:

- as an alternative to a traditional textbook in a class where you'd like to experiment with not using a textbook or using an affordable or free one

- as a supplement (a "TL;DR" version, if you will) to a traditional textbook

- as a self-study guide, a kind of manual or handbook students might use on their own time

- as a way for you to have students explore some ideas about what writing is and what it should do at the university level, by discussing whether you, as their instructor, agree with the way various themes are presented and having students reflect on some of the claims made in the book

- as a reference guide to specific topics, where you give out one or two sections as needed while teaching a specific thing, like summarizing or attribution.

Feel free to assign just a few chapters or sections here and there and in whatever order you want – this book could have been organized a thousand different ways, so let your own needs and those of your students guide how you use it.

I hope you find this book at least somewhat helpful, and I hope you feel free to disagree with it and tell your students why, because in doing so, you'll prove something that will be useful to them: that not everyone agrees on what good writing is and how it's done, and that this is an important fact they'll need to navigate throughout their academic careers. Oh – and also, there's an appendix at the end of the book with some ideas for activities you might consider using or adapting.

 TL;DR: This is a very short book about academic writing. I hope you like it, but you don't have to.

Preface

I want to tell you a little something about the title of this book. *TL;DR* means "too long; didn't read." It's a thing people say on the internet when they run into a giant block of text that looks long and boring.

Actually, that's not totally true: it's usually the writer of the giant block themselves who ends a long, rambling post with something like the following:

the entire text of Moby-Dick
⚡ TL;DR: A guy chases a whale for a long time.

To be honest, "a giant block of text that looks long and boring" describes what textbooks can feel like sometimes. It also describes what some people think their papers should look like in university.

I'm here to tell you this doesn't have to be the case.

This book is called *TL;DR* because there's a lot you need to know about writing and reading in university, but it can sometimes be boring to read about. I decided to write a very short guide that includes everything I think is important, explained as clearly and simply as possible. My hope is no one will have to say "TL;DR" about this book. There are very few references, not many detailed examples, no exercises, and no assignments. Just stuff you as a student should know.

Also, I know that sometimes it can feel like everything is too long to read, and that you need to write long, dense papers with a whole lot of long, fancy words, in long, fancy sentences, in long, fancy paragraphs. But there are ways to approach long texts that can make them easier to read, and there are ways to write that are simpler, more concise, and easier than you might think.

Why should you trust me, the person who is going to be giving you supposedly good advice throughout this book, if you don't know me? I've been teaching writing for a long time. I think I know what works and what doesn't. And I'm here to help.

The more I think about it, the more I think trust is a really important ingredient in the whole university experience.

First and foremost, we (your professors and instructors) owe it to you. If you can't trust us – trust that we know what we're doing and we really want to help you do well at the stuff we are teaching – then we're not doing our jobs well.

I hope you know that most of us do strive to be trustworthy, and that we really do want to see you succeed, even if it feels like we're just randomly giving out grades sometimes. At the same time, trust needs to be mutual: you have to be able to trust your peers, and your peers and instructors have to be able to trust you. I don't just mean that we all have to be able to trust that nobody is cheating (though that surely is important), but we have to be able to trust at a much more basic, human level that we're going to do our best to meet commitments we've made, do the work we've signed up to do, and do it with kindness and respect.

We'll fail each other sometimes, but there's a kind of unwritten contract that we've all got to try to do our best at this, even if it's a class we kind of don't want to take (for students) or teach (for instructors).

It's in that spirit that I offer this short book.

 TL;DR: Writing doesn't have to be hard, but we have to be nice to each other.

TL;DR

Introduction

Universities are ABOUT writing.

—Ken Hyland, "Writing in the University"

Writing is the most important thing in the world.

OK, maybe not. But it's definitely *one* of the most important.

You don't have to think writing is fun or interesting, but it has changed the world more than almost any other human technology. It has created countries, started wars, made laws, brought about liberation and oppression. It's hard to think of any other thing humans have made that has changed the world more, including the internet and nuclear weapons.

It also seems completely magical to me. Did you know that with language we have finite resources – a limited number of words available to us – but that by combining and adding things to our sentences, using simple tools of grammar we all know simply from having grown up listening to language, we can make sentences go on and on *literally forever?*

3

I'm not saying we *should* make sentences go forever. I'm just saying it's pretty amazing that we *can*.

Writing is a big deal in many – perhaps most – contemporary cultures and societies, and it's almost definitely a big deal in the context you find yourself, which is probably a university.

Writing well, or at least being able to write in a way that's effective for your purpose, is going to be important for you during university, and maybe for the rest of your life. Your writing will be evaluated a lot for the next few years, and more importantly, you'll use writing to learn, think, and understand. And it can be a very useful tool for doing all of those things.

"Writing well" for the next few years might look different than what you've gotten used to in your life so far. This book is meant to tell you some basic information about how to "write well" in a simple, short, and easy-to-read way. I'm going to try to say in a few short chapters what a lot of textbooks try to explain in two hundred or three hundred or five hundred pages.

There aren't many examples or references in this book – not because they aren't helpful, but because I want to be as direct as possible. The book doesn't address every single problem you'll face when it comes to writing, and it doesn't explain how to write every type of assignment. It's just quick, easy, bite-sized chunks of advice that I think you'll find helpful as you navigate your first couple of years of academic writing after high school.

I will provide a very short summary at the end of each section, like this:

 TL;DR: Writing is really important in our society, and this short book will give you some (hopefully) good advice about how to do it while you're in university.

ONE

Stuff You Should Know before You Start

Literacy

Reading is not exhausted merely by decoding the written word or written language, but rather anticipated by and extending into knowledge of the world.

—Paulo Freire, "The Importance of the Act of Reading"

You Are Already Good at Reading and Writing

Sometimes when we talk about reading and writing, we use the word *literacy*. Even though they have the same root word, literacy has nothing to do with literature. Literacy just means reading and writing – and not just poetry or novels or whatever, but grocery lists and emails and text messages and road signs.

Since the 1990s or so, the meaning of literacy has expanded to include other things like visual design, sound, video, and so on.

My own fancy academic definition of literacy is "any symbolic meaning-making activity."

This sounds complicated, but we all do it all the time. If you're like most undergraduates, you have been super into literacy for most of your life. Using social media and texting are all literacy activities. You are probably good at using some of them because you've had a lot of practice.

Maybe a better definition is "being able to understand or make sense of something."

Communicating using social media or your phone or computer is one kind of literacy, and the reading and writing you have done in school for most of your life is another kind. So is being able to read a poster advertising a concert or knowing what the traffic signals at a stoplight mean. All of these things are different, but it's all symbolic meaning-making activity. It's all making sense of or understanding things by using language and other symbols.

TL;DR: Literacy just means knowing how to do things, usually with words.

There Are Different Kinds of Literacy

The language we use in school is not better or more special than other kinds of language; it's just different. This is over-simplified, but some people would break it down like this:

Out of school	In school
Informal	Formal
Simple words	Complicated words
Short and simple sentences	Long and complicated sentences
Connected to real life	Connected to abstract ideas
More oral or speech-like	More written or book-like

Out of school	In school
Playful, fun, sometimes rude	Serious and proper (no swear words!)
Progressive; new words and slang	Conservative; traditional
Grammar and spelling don't matter	Grammar and spelling matter a lot
Your family's language or dialect	English only

It isn't always this black and white. The reality of literacy is always more complicated. Depending on what you want to say, you might mix some stuff from the out-of-school side with the in-school side when you write in one class or another. That's often OK, and it will usually be clear if your prof is OK with it. For example, some assignments might call for "personal reflection," which would probably be less formal than a paper written using information you found in academic journal articles.

It's important to know that some of your professors will feel very strongly that only the stuff on the right side of the chart is OK. They're probably remembering what they were taught, but the truth is, there are a lot of different ways to write successfully, depending on who you're writing for and what they expect. The important thing – and this is the first of many times I will repeat this – is to learn about what your reader (in this case, usually your prof or TA) wants or expects.

I had a student a few years ago who would repeat variations on the same phrase whenever we met to discuss her papers: "What are you looking for here?" "I'm not sure what you're looking for here." "I didn't know what you were looking for there." I'll be honest: at first, I found this a bit annoying. But she was right to be so persistent. I really had to explain *what* I thought was important for the assignment, and I had to explain *why*. It was as hard for me as it was for her, but it made her paper better, and made me a better teacher.

It's important to find out if your instructor feels strongly that your writing needs to stay on the in-school side of this oversimplified chart. If you disagree with them, you have a couple of choices. You can try to write that way, or you can try to get them to change their minds by writing things that are good but break their rules. (A warning: you do this at your own risk. Not every instructor is interested in reading groundbreaking, experimental writing, which is why it's important that you get to know them and their expectations.)

It's true that what most people call "academic writing" looks more like the in-school side of the chart, but some of the stuff on the right side is less important than it seems.

For example, complicated words and long sentences don't often make academic writing better. Usually, it's better to be simple and direct. Don't go out of your way to use "fancy" words just because you think it will make you sound smart. Sometimes the simplicity and directness of the out-of-school side are perfectly OK for a university writing assignment. As I said, it depends on the situation.

 TL;DR: You can write however you want, but many profs will prefer formal language. However, you may be able to break the "rules" if and when you want.

Reading and Writing in University Is Different Than in High School

In most high schools, there is a class called English (or Language Arts) that includes all kinds of things having to do with language – things like spelling, grammar, vocabulary, poetry, creative writing, and literature.

However, unless you're taking an English literature class in university, things like literature and poetry *don't* have much of a relationship to academic writing at all. You don't need to write in a "poetic" style to be a good academic writer.

In high school English, you might have learned about figurative language – metaphors, similes, and things like that. You might have learned that you need to use this kind of language to make your writing interesting or beautiful. You might have also learned that you need a fun "hook" to get readers interested in your introduction.

In university, you don't usually need any of those things. It depends on what you're studying, but in university, the following things are usually more important in writing:

- understanding the expectations of your audience (usually your professor)

- being direct about what you intend to communicate

- carefully and clearly explaining how you're using other texts

- having a clear main purpose or thesis for a piece of writing

- writing paragraphs that have one main focus

- writing with words and sentence patterns that fit the purpose

- producing a text that is relatively free of grammar errors.

You might try thinking of writing as a tool for doing things rather than as an art form.

It can be (and is) both, of course. But if you learned that writing is poetry in high school, try thinking of writing as more like a screwdriver in university. Writing can be Shakespeare, yes, but it can also be a user manual for your wireless headphones – a tool to accomplish a purpose.

 TL;DR: Unlike other kinds of writing, academic writing doesn't have to be beautiful or fancy; it should be clear and direct.

Language

Academic writing is a second language for everyone.

—Ling Shi, during a class I took from her

You Don't Have to Write Like a "Native Speaker"

If you grew up speaking a language other than English at home, and you learned English in school, you might think you're at a disadvantage at an "English-speaking" university. This isn't true! If you studied English as a second or additional language, you probably have *more* knowledge of English grammar than your classmates who grew up only speaking English, because you probably had to learn all the rules.

It's true that there are certain patterns or variations that are more common to so-called ESL writers, but it doesn't make them wrong.

In fact, "standard" English is mostly an imaginary language hardly anyone uses.

Your writing teacher will definitely point out serious errors in grammar or word choice or sentence structure if you make them, but not all variations from so-called standard English are actually wrong. They're just different.

So-called native speakers do this all the time too. Being a native speaker doesn't make you automatically better at writing in English in school. It just means English is the language you grew up with. Nobody grows up writing ten-page academic papers with APA-style reference lists, though. (And if you did, that's weird. I'm sorry.)

If you're worried about making errors, consider keeping track of all the errors that your professors mark. I know that sounds like a lot of work, and it probably will be. You can write them all down in a notebook or on a spreadsheet or something. You can note what the error was, and what the correct version of it would be. Go back to it every few weeks and look for patterns. Is there something that comes up over and over? Try to focus on that.

If you find English grammar confusing, or find it very hard to write English sentences: first, you're not alone, and second, unfortunately, there's no magical way to suddenly improve in a few days or weeks. You're probably going to have to do a lot of reading and writing in English for a long time. It's hard, but if you keep at it, you'll find yourself getting more comfortable and eventually notice real improvement.

 TL;DR: Not being a "native speaker" doesn't mean you're a bad writer.

Racism, Prejudice, and Judgments about Language

Another thing to be aware of: it's OK to break rules some-times, even the rules of so-called standard English. Some people call this writing with an "accent," but the fact is we all have ways of using language that feel more right and true and useful to us and that might not always match the grammar or vocabulary of standard English.

The way I'm writing this book is a good example of breaking the rules. When I sat down to write this, I decided I was going to ignore what many people have been telling me my whole life: that my sentences are sometimes too "wordy," or that I overuse *I,* or that I should stop using so many adverbs like *basically* or *totally* or *entirely.* But I like writing that way, and even though I try to change those things when I write more formal academic articles, I feel like it will make this book more readable and personable. (I hope I'm right.)

"But Joel," you might say, even though we don't really know each other, "you're a middle-aged white guy. When you break the rules, people seem to be OK with it, but what about me, who is not a middle-aged white guy?"

And I would say, "You're right to bring this up, and also, I feel like you should've said 'who *am* not a middle-aged white guy,' but now that I think about it, that doesn't sound right either. English grammar is weird."

Grammar aside, this question is absolutely a relevant and important one. What happens when, say, a young

South Asian woman or Black man breaks "the rules" of writing? There are linguistic judgments made that are not actually based on language but on what some linguists call "raciolinguistics." To give one brief disturbing example: There are research studies in which people are asked to rate a speaker's English after listening to a recording and seeing a picture of the person who is (supposedly) speaking. Sometimes their rating of how good the speaker's English is changes depending on the race of the person whose picture is shown – even when the recordings are actually of the same person, but the pictures are different. That is, people may rate a racialized person's English as "worse" than a white person's even when they sound identical.

There are convincing arguments to be made that an insistence on strictly following certain norms of so-called standard English (which, to be totally honest, doesn't really exist except as an imagined concept people use to complain about language they don't like) is part of upholding systemic racism and contributes to the marginalization of already marginalized peoples' ways of using language. Not everyone agrees with this perspective, and I'm in no position to tell you how to think about this issue, because I don't have the same life experience as you. But it's worth knowing and being aware that people often use words like *correctness, norms,* and *standards* when they're really making judgments based on race.

TL;DR: Many people make judgments about students' writing based not on the quality of language but on racial stereotypes and prejudices.

Audience

The writer's audience is always a fiction.

—Walter J. Ong

You Are Writing for Your Professor, Mostly

It's important to think of your audience and purpose in writing. The most obvious audience for university writing is your professor or TA, the person who gave you the assignment or who will grade it. And the "purpose" is that that person told you to write the paper.

I realize that this can make the whole thing feel kind of fake.

Some writing has an obvious real-world purpose. The purpose of a research article is to communicate knowledge. The purpose of a news article on a sports website is to tell you who won the game. The purpose of an Instagram caption is to tell you about Kim Kardashian's new perfume, or whatever. These are real-world things that those writers and their texts are *doing*.

So what is the purpose of, say, your lab report? It does have some connection to the real world. You need to explain what you did during your lab experiment, which is, indeed, a real thing that happened in the real world. (I'm not a scientist, so I don't really know what you're doing in the lab, but I'm sure it was cool!)

But there's another purpose that isn't talked about as much, and it's not related to the "real world" so much as its "meta"-purpose, a purpose beyond the stated aim of the assignment. It's for you to show your instructor that you understood the assignment, that you know the proper names for the things you're learning about, and that you can write about them in a way that other people familiar with that subject can understand and make sense of.

In a way, then, the hidden purpose of every writing assignment in university is to "prove you can write this kind of assignment." That does feel a bit artificial, but it isn't all bad. This is actually an important part of the thing you're learning to do in university: to develop your knowledge and skills – your literacy, really – in the subject(s) you're studying.

Even though this audience (your prof) and purpose (prove you understood the assignment) can feel artificial, you should still take it seriously and recognize that it's important. You need to know your professor's preferences and what they think good writing is. "Understanding the assignment" will turn out to be a pretty crucial skill throughout university, in your career, and even in your relationships with other people throughout your life.

To "understand the assignment" *is* the assignment. Learning different ways of doing things (in this case, writing) that are called for (or useful, or helpful) in different situations is one of the most important things about being human.

Sometimes professors will be clear about the purposes they have in mind, and they will give you clear directions for how to complete assignments and explain their expectations. Sometimes they won't do this at all, and you'll have to push a bit, like my student did with me ("What are you looking for here?") or you'll need to look elsewhere for help and advice, like a friend or a writing centre.

If you don't like this more artificial purpose ("prove you understand the assignment") – and I don't blame you! – it can also help to have in mind an imaginary third party as your audience rather than just the person grading your paper. It could be your classmates, or people who also study the subject you're studying, or someone else. Your professor might even directly tell you who your imaginary audience should be.

This imaginary audience is actually kind of real, because you make it real. If you write with that audience in mind, it will change what you write. If you imagine you're writing for an audience of doctors, you may find you naturally choose different language than if you imagine you're writing for your uncle who posts outdated memes on Facebook. The better you know your audience – real or imagined – the better chance you have to tell them what you want to tell them.

 TL;DR: Write for your professor or an imaginary audience you think would be interested in what you're writing about.

Genre

We don't write writing, we write *something*.

—Anthony Paré, "What We Know about Writing,
and Why It Matters"

There's No Such Thing as "Just Writing"

Genre is a French word that means "kind" or "type." It's sort of like a category for art or language or other things humans produce.

Punk is a genre of music; horror is a genre of movies; romance is a genre of novels.

Genres are collections of features that we have come to expect in a given situation; they are ways of organizing human activity. How do we know what the features of a genre are? Usually, we know a genre from being a part of our larger culture and being exposed to it and told what it is by other people. We may know punk rock has distorted guitars and fast drums and loud shouted vocals. But if you don't know the culture, you might not know the genres. I know nothing about music like EDM or IDM (I think they both mean a kind of dance music?) or chillwave (I couldn't even tell you one feature of this genre, or even if people still listen to it, but I've heard people talk about it). And if you're new to university, you probably aren't too familiar with the common genres of texts in academia.

Academic writing has many different genres. This is one of the reasons it can be hard to get a handle on "how to write" in university, because you're probably being asked to write many different types of things.

A researcher called Michael Carter came up with a useful set of categories that he calls "metagenres," or types of writing that might include many other types. In his article "Ways of Knowing, Doing, and Writing in the Disciplines," he shows that four metagenres are usually called for in university, depending on the purpose you're writing for:

1 *problem-solving or system-generating texts* (business, nursing, social work, engineering). This could be a response to a business case study or an explanation of how something works to accompany a diagram in an engineering text.

2 *empirical inquiry texts* (science, medicine, social sciences). This could be a paper about a chemistry experiment, the results of survey research, or a write-up of a clinical trial.

3 *research from written sources* (humanities). This is a pretty common one to encounter early in your under-grad career: often it's a paper making an argument

about a literary text, but it could be about almost anything. See Chapter 3, "Writing 'The Paper.'"

4 *performance or critique of a performance* (arts). This could be a spoken-word performance or a review of a film or a play or a concert.

There might be different names for specific versions of these genres; you might write a lab report (no. 2) or conduct a survey and write up the results in a research article (also no. 2). You might write an analysis of a poem (no. 3) or a description of a historical event (also no. 3).

The stuff that you learn to write in your "writing class" doesn't always match the stuff you go on to write in your "real classes." Again, this might feel a little artificial, but the hope is that it will be useful later on. For example, in a class I teach, we have a stand-alone summary assignment, where students have to write short summaries of a variety of types of texts. You might not have another professor tell you to "write a summary" in, say, a third-year psychology course, but you might find that *part* of the paper calls for doing just that.

No matter what the class, your job is to try to figure out what you're being asked to write. If you're not sure *how* to write a certain assignment, or what genre it's supposed to be, read the assignment or syllabus carefully, or ask your professor or writing centre for examples of other pieces of writing in that genre. If you can, try to start a discussion about what they consider to be features of a good assignment of this type, or try to find models of successful papers while gently asking, "What is it, exactly, you're looking for here?"

 TL;DR: Different classes and assignments call for different genres; genres are ways of putting texts together that different cultures (or fields or disciplines, etc.) have developed expectations for.

TWO

Reading and Writing about Other Texts

Academic Reading

Read everything.

—Paul Kei Matsuda

First of all: I know that you already know how to read.

Like writing, reading is a bit different in university than it is outside of it. The texts you read in university courses are likely longer and more complex, and might be hard to read (or boring, to be honest) at first. If the thing you're reading is an introductory textbook, the author is probably an expert who is trying to get a lot of information across to you in a short space, and it might feel overwhelming. If it's an article from an academic journal, the author is usually a researcher who knows so much about their subject that the only people who can really understand them are other experts in that field, which is who their intended audience usually is.

Read before You Read

A good way to start is what some people call "prereading" or "reading around" a text. You should start by reading everything but the actual text. If you've got a journal article, read the title, the author's name, and the name of the journal. If it's got an abstract, read that, and read it carefully. The abstract is a short paragraph before a research article that gives you a summary of the whole thing. It's almost always useful. It will tell you all the important information in the text. (In fact, if you're in a hurry you can *just* read the abstract, but don't tell your professor I said that.) Then read any section headings that are in the text, and if you have time, skim the introduction and conclusion. If you've got a textbook chapter to read, look at the whole table of contents to see where the chapter fits, read all the headings and subheadings in the chapter, look at the pictures, charts, and diagrams, and, again, skim the intro and conclusion.

Then ask yourself what you know about the text before you start reading it. Hopefully, you have some idea of the academic field the text is a part of, who wrote the text and why they wrote it, and what the general focus or purpose of the text is. This context might be part of how your prof introduced the reading, but if it isn't, you can look for those things on your own.

Write While You Read

You should get in the habit of taking notes while you read. A lot of people think writing notes by hand on actual paper is the best way to do this, and I agree, but it's OK if you don't have any paper. It's helpful to make little notes in the margins; you can summarize as you read to help you remember what each section or paragraph or part is about. You may also want to make notes of things you agree or disagree with, things that confuse you or make you angry, or questions you have about something the author claimed. All this will help you take in the text, understand it, and process it, so your notes will be useful when you start writing about it.

Something that can be helpful is making a "reverse outline." Usually, an outline is a rough sketch or plan of the different parts of a paper you plan to write, and it's usually written before you start writing the actual paper, or around the time you start writing. The reverse outline is the same – a rough sketch of the different parts of the text – but it's written *after* you have read a complete text. If you're reading something dense or difficult and want to keep everything straight in your head, try writing a short summary – usually not even a complete sentence – of the main ideas of each paragraph or couple of paragraphs in the margins of the text. This might help you retain the information better and remind you how the writer's ideas fit together.

Really, though, it's OK if you don't understand everything you read. Ideally, you'll be able to make it through a text without stopping every few seconds to look up a word or a concept; you can make notes of things you need to clarify and then look them up, or perhaps even better, talk to a classmate or ask about it on your class group chat, if you have one. Meanings can become clearer when we try to learn them along with other people.

TL;DR: Do a lot of skimming before you start reading to get some idea of what a text is going to do, and always take notes while you read.

Summary

Let me explain. No, there is too much – let me sum up.

—Mandy Patinkin as Indigo Montoya in *The Princess Bride*

Explaining Another Text

Summarizing means explaining what another text is about in "your own words." I put *your own words* in quotes because what are "your own words" anyway? (See the sections on paraphrasing and plagiarism for more on this.) So, for now, let's talk about some basic rules for writing a summary.

Overall, your summary should briefly answer these questions: What was that text mostly about? What was its main idea, point, or argument?

Here are four things to keep in mind when summarizing:

Be objective and accurate. You need to accurately and objectively tell your reader what the text was mainly about. This means that there's not much room for you to express your own reactions to the text (unless your professor wants you to); your main task is to get the information across. Even if you disagree with the author, it's important to present their views or ideas accurately rather than going into detail about why you think they're wrong.

Be thorough but concise. Ideally, you should imagine that the reader has not read the text you're summarizing, so you'll usually need to explain things like the names and significance of people or organizations mentioned in the text. So don't just say the text is about "Dr. Smith, who works with the ABCDE organization"; let the reader know it's Josephine Smith, a researcher at (let's say) the University of Alaska, and she works with the Association of Broccoli, Carrot, and Daikon Enthusiasts.[*]

At the same time, you don't need to mention a lot of small details that don't serve the main focus or purpose of the original text. Maybe the original author mentioned Dr. Smith's dog in one sentence; unless the article is mostly about dogs, you can leave the dog out.[†]

Provide context. Don't just jump right into reporting "the facts." Your readers need to know where this information is coming from. Provide some sense of who wrote the article and what the overall vibe is; where it fits in the larger world of the thing the author is writing about.

---

[*] I'm sorry for that weird example. This is why I don't use a lot of examples.

[†] Again, sorry.

Attribute words and ideas to their authors. This is a big one: use phrases like "according to [author's name]…" or "[author] claims that…" or "Finally, [author] explains that…" *a lot.* Use them *way* more than you think you need to. If you don't attribute almost everything to the original author, the reader most likely won't know where this stuff came from, and in many cases may assume you're claiming these are your words and ideas. We will talk about this in detail in the next few pages.

 TL;DR: Summaries should be mostly objective, thorough, concise, and clearly attributed to the person who wrote the text you're summarizing.

Attribution

You miss 100 percent of the shots
you don't take – Wayne Gretzky.

—Michael Scott, *The Office**

Why Attribution Matters

Information isn't a neutral thing just floating around out there. It's part of a larger social and cultural world. This is why it's important to distinguish your "voice" as the writer of the summary from the voice of the author in the original text. You didn't make all this information up; it came from somewhere else.

But wait – didn't the last section say you should be "objective" in a summary? Why are we talking about your voice, then?

---

* This is a joke from the American TV show *The Office*, but if you've never seen it or don't know who Wayne Gretzky is, it needs a little explaining. The joke is that while Wayne Gretzky, who many people consider the greatest hockey player of all time, really did say this, the character in the show, Michael Scott, is attributing the quote to Gretzky, which is accurate and correct, but he's also attributing it to himself, which just makes this whole thing confusing.

By *voice,* I don't mean your opinions or views. When you're just summarizing, it's true that those things are often not useful or called for.

What I mean is this: in academic writing, you often have to remind your reader that you're the one putting together information from a variety of sources.

Here's what is happening in the chain of communicating this information:

You're not a journalist or researcher on the ground, reporting events or ideas first-hand; you're the middleman, the mediator between the original text and your reader.

This might sound strange, but the best way to show that you have a voice as a summarizer is to use attribution to show that you're not the original author – make it clear to your reader that you're not the person who discovered or created the information to begin with. Paradoxically, if you use a lot of attribution, you create a *new* voice for yourself. Rather than positioning yourself as the neutral conduit of neutral information (which doesn't really exist, remember!) you create an identity as the understander, the messenger, or the interpreter of the original text or texts, passing on the important information to the reader through the lens of your own reading.

Two Types of Attribution

The most obvious type of attribution you'll do is to the original author of a text you read, as discussed in the last section ("The author says X," "The author claims X," etc.). (By the way, you may be in the habit of literally writing the words *the author,* but in higher-level academic writing, it's much more common to refer to the author by their name, which we'll touch on in a minute.)

However, you may also need to do a kind of "secondary" attribution to people the author mentioned and attributed ideas to in the original text. The author of the text *you* read and are summarizing wasn't just sharing their own ideas; they probably borrowed some words and ideas from other people. And now it's your job not only to show what you're borrowing from them, but what they borrowed from others.

When that happens, the chain of communicating information looks like this:

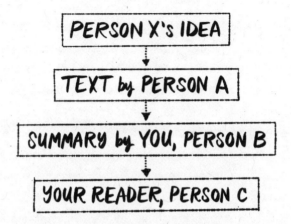

This is getting complicated, I know. Now you have to communicate to your reader that what they're getting is fourth-hand information: Person C (the reader) is learning about Person X's idea through Person B (you) explaining how Person A wrote about it.

How can we do this kind of attribution? Different style guides have rules about what's called "secondary citations," but the basic form turns out not to be too hard:

Person A explains that Person X's argument is...

Person A interviewed Person X, who claimed that...

Person A uses Person X's concept of [whatever] to show how...

Boom.

Using the Author's Name, Not Just "the Author"

Some people get in the habit of referring to the writer of a text as "the author." This might be something that is taught in high school, or it might just be a habit because it's simple and easy to do. It's not wrong, but it's also not precise. Chances are you'll be writing papers that include information that comes from a wide variety of authors and texts, and in this case, referring to the writer of a text simply as "the author" will be confusing.

Different style guides have different ways of referring to writers (more on this in a later section), but you can't go wrong with using the writer's actual name almost every time you want to refer to them or attribute an idea to them. I tell my students to use the writer's real name in most sentences of a summary, even if it feels repetitive, and I almost always advise against using the phrase *the author* except in cases of multiauthored papers, where it can get tiresome to repeat several names over and over. In that case, I usually advise something like this:

Heng Hartse and Kubota (2014) have a different view. Although the authors acknowledge the complexities of this phenomenon, they also argue that ...

Here, I've used the authors' actual last names (in APA style), referred to them as "the authors," and used the pronoun *they* rather than repeating their names. If I continued to refer to Heng Hartse and Kubota's 2014 paper in this paragraph, I would probably employ this same mix of words again, but I would use the actual names more often than *the authors*.

 TL;DR: You should explain that you're using other peoples' ideas as clearly as you can, usually by mentioning their names a lot. Like a *lot*.

Paraphrasing and Quotation

We defined *paraphrasing* as restating a passage
from a source in fresh language, though sometimes
with keywords retained from that passage.

—Rebecca Moore Howard, Tricia Serviss,
and Tanya K. Rodrigue,
"Writing from Sources, Writing from Sentences"

How to Refer to Other People's Words and Ideas

Some writing guides lump "paraphrasing, summary, and quotation" together as three ways of explaining other texts. Really, paraphrasing and quotation are two tools you can use while doing the larger project of summarizing.

Paraphrasing is writing about the original author's ideas using language that is *similar* enough to the original to give your reader the information they need but *different* enough that it shows the reader that you understood and processed the original text. (Remember, your audience, whoever else you might imagine, is ultimately your professor, and they want to know that you're learning the material.)

Quotation is using the *exact same* words, sentences, and structures as the original author, and putting those words inside quotation marks. That's these little guys:

" "

Using Quotations

How much quotation should you use in a summary? Not a lot. It depends, but maybe no more than about ten to twenty percent of your whole text should be quotes. In general, it's best to quote only technical explanations, or definitions of key concepts, or short passages that you think are so powerful or well-written that you feel the reader really needs to see them.

It's important to integrate quotes into your own sentences or paragraphs in a way that explains them in context – you shouldn't just drop a quote into your paper with no explanation. Here's a quick example. Let's say a student is using a quote from a short story by the writer C.D.B. Bryan called "So Much Unfairness of Things" (1962), which is about a kid who gets kicked out of a private high school.

NO **Sometimes it's hard to learn important lessons. "You will *never* be able to look back on this and laugh. But you may be able to understand."**
⚡ There's no explanation about where the quote comes from, who wrote or said it, or why it's being used here.

BETTER Sometimes it's hard to learn important lessons. As C.D.B. Bryan wrote in 1962, "You will *never* be able to look back on this and laugh. But you may be able to understand."

⚡ This helps, because at least we know where the quote comes from, but it's still not clearly connected to whatever the student is writing about.

EVEN BETTER Sometimes it's hard to learn important lessons. Although we may not "be able to look back" on our mistakes "and laugh," as C.D.B. Bryan wrote in "So Much Unfairness of Things" in 1962, we "may be able to understand" the consequences of our actions in hindsight.

⚡ The quote is really chopped up here, which might seem strange if you're not used to doing it, but it's perfectly acceptable to do this in academic writing, and often it's a good strategy. The goal is to integrate the quote into the "flow" of your own sentences and ideas. We will talk about this a bit more in the next section when we get to the concept of using sources.

Paraphrasing

Most of your summary should be paraphrasing. Paraphrasing is "using your own words," which you have heard about in school for most of your life. What this does *not* mean is the method you might call "using mostly the same words as the original text but changing a few of the important words."

If you got into the habit of doing this, you'll need to stop, because this is really not OK in university. At best, it's seen as unsophisticated; worse, it's seen as lazy; and at worst it's seen as a serious form of plagiarism or cheating. (We will talk about plagiarism more soon, but I feel like I should really stress this: sometimes what people think of as paraphrasing before they get to university is a lot closer to what university professors think of as plagiarism.)

Paraphrasing, at its best, involves making major changes in things like which words you use, what order they are in, what forms those words are in, and how they're put into sentences.

Here's a quick example using the second sentence of this section, "Really, paraphrasing and quotation are two tools you can use while doing the larger project of summarizing."

1 **Truly, paraphrasing and quotation are two things you can use while doing the bigger project of summarizing.**

2 **Your main project is writing a summary, and there are two strategies you can use to do that: one is paraphrasing the original text, the other is quoting some of its exact words.**

You can see that no. 1 is pretty much the exact same sentence as the original text, with a few words changed or removed. No. 2 rearranges the information, changes most (but not all!) of the words, and even adds some additional context. No. 2 is much better.

Generally, if you see yourself using more than three or four words in a row from the original, you should check and see if there's another way to rearrange things or change words. Or you can decide to go ahead and use the exact words, but as a quotation.

TL;DR: Summarizing includes paraphrasing, which means presenting the same information but in a *very* different arrangement of words, and a bit of quotation, which means using the exact same words from the original, in quotation marks.

Response

I write entirely to find out what I'm thinking,
what I'm looking at, what I see and what it means.

—Joan Didion, "Why I Write"

Telling Readers What You Think about Other Texts
Even though the last few pages talk about summaries as if they're always 100 percent objective and your opinion doesn't matter, most assignments do involve some subjectivity – that is, providing your own perspective in some way. There are a lot of different ways to describe what we do when we provide our perspective on other texts. After you read something, you may be asked to do one of the following:

- respond to
- critique
- criticize
- reflect on
- analyze
- evaluate.

Whatever your professor calls it, you may encounter assignments in which you're asked to say what you think about something. But you have to do this in a way that balances your "objective" summary, which shows you understand and can explain the text (the things we talked about in the last few sections), with your own reactions to it.

First, should you use the word *I* and phrases like "I think" or "in my opinion" in your text? Despite what many high school teachers teach, *I* is used in high-level academic writing all the time but is less common in some fields than others. You can probably tell, for example, from the way I've been using it in this book that I think it's totally fine to use *I* in some contexts, because, I think, it makes the writer seem maybe more friendly or trustworthy or honest or personal. (I mean, I hope so!)

Don't try to come up with weird ways to wiggle around *I* if you can't or don't want to use it; just say what you think. (Like, instead of "I think dogs are awesome," just write "dogs are awesome.") As usual, you need to get to know the person who's grading your assignments to know how OK it is.

Regardless of whether you use *I,* what exactly should you be reacting *to?* Usually, I recommend two different approaches: responding to ideas and arguments, and responding to how the ideas are communicated.

Responding to ideas and arguments. This is where you can be direct about agreeing or disagreeing with whatever main point or points the text is making. I'm going to do an imaginary example here, so bear with me.

Let's say the original text is by someone called Gerald Bookman (I just made him up), and one sentence in it says,

More people are reading e-books today than ever before, and it's time for publishers to consider phasing out print books entirely.

I love books, and I would hate to see them die, so if this were me, I know that at some point I would just come out and say it, in maybe one of these ways:

"I disagree with Bookman."
⚡ You can't get much more direct than that.

"Bookman is wrong."
⚡ Again – very clear.

"While e-books may be gaining popularity, print books should not be abandoned."
⚡ This one is a bit longer, and you'll notice I didn't really make an evaluative judgment of his argument – I just stated a claim that is opposed to the one he made.

Any of these might be a good place to start, but I can't stop here, because I haven't explained *why* I disagree, or why anybody should listen to what I have to say about this. Someone could easily reply with a quote from the classic nineties film *The Big Lebowski:* "That's just, like, your *opinion,* man."

In other words, you've got to be sure you have something that can do one of the following to your position:

- back it up

- support it

- give evidence for it

- explain it.

Don't stop at "I agree" or "I disagree." You need to tell the reader why you responded the way you did.

What is an acceptable answer to this *why?* In some cases, the why will need to have hard evidence behind it, like statistics, or information from empirical research; many times, especially in an assignment I call "The Paper," which we'll talk about in the next chapter, you'll usually refer to the work of other authors, scholars, or experts whose positions align more with your own. In some cases, you may be able to write mainly based on your own life experiences or deeply held beliefs, or simply try to create a convincing hypothetical or imagined example that has the ring of truth.

Responding to how ideas are communicated. This can be trickier, but it's sometimes better to do than simply saying, "I disagree."

If you want to explain why you think the writer made their point in a way that was not effective, or problematic, or ignorant, you can draw attention to the problems with their evidence, reasons, explanations, and so on. This can involve things like pointing out that the writer has failed to consider other perspectives and what those perspectives might add, or pointing out that something in the author's argument doesn't make sense or isn't fair, or that they didn't mention something that would be important to consider when thinking about the issue under discussion.

There are other things you can do, but these – responding to the argument and responding to the way the author made their argument – are two of the most direct and simplest things you can do when responding to a text. Depending on how you feel about the point the original text made, you can choose one, or you can do a combination of both.

A Note about Agreeing with the Original Text

Somehow, this feels harder to do well. Maybe it's because we're taught that "critical thinking" is important when we respond to ideas, and we think being critical means we have to be negative or disagree. If your professor gives you a text to respond to, and you think pretty much everything in it seems 100 percent right, but you still have to write five hundred words, what are you supposed to do? Just write "I agree with Bookman" over and over? Probably not. I suggest using a modified version of the disagreement-type strategies mentioned above – you can still provide reasons and evidence in support of the position of the original text, and, in fact, you'll have a lot of things from the text itself to borrow from. (Not that you want to repeat everything they said exactly, but you can highlight parts that seem especially strong and explain why they're so convincing, from your own perspective.)

You can also do what Gerald Graff and Cathy Birkenstein talk about in their book, *They Say / I Say,* which is to respond with, "OK, but..." This is a kind of agreement with a twist. You might agree with some parts of what the original text said, but not all of it.

This gives you the chance to explain your own position more directly, but keep in mind the genre of the assignment. If the main goal is to critically respond to the original text, you should keep your response rooted in the text, bringing up your multisided agreement-disagreement in relation to specific points made in the text. Try not to go too far down the path of offering your opinion about something only partially related to the original text, however. I've seen a few "response" papers that make this mistake. The writer might begin, "I agree with Bookman that e-books have many advantages, but paper books are better for children," which sounds interesting, but then they go on to write several paragraphs about how technology has been harmful to children and talk about television, smartphones, YouTube, and many other unrelated things until the question of print books has vanished altogether.

So don't do that, but do feel free to have a more nuanced, double-sided approach, if that's what makes sense to you – as long as you keep your response directly related to the original text's points. (Maybe you can refer back to that reverse outline you made of the text while you were reading it. You did do that, right?)

TL;DR: Many assignments ask for your response to another text, which you can do by directly agreeing or disagreeing with or critiquing the original writer's argument (with evidence to back up your view). Make sure that what you do is grounded in the things the original text says, not just whatever was already in your head before you started reading.

Stance

Here I stand; I can do no other.

—Martin Luther*

Using Language to Show Your Position

The last section may have made it sound as if every text you respond to will be an argumentative one, and that you might have an argument to make in response to it. This isn't strictly true, even if it can be a good way to think about approaching this kind of assignment. I don't even like to use the word *argument* when I talk about responding to texts, because *argument* sounds like a knock-down, drag-out fight where you explain why your view is absolutely correct and why anyone who disagrees with you is a big dumb idiot.

That's how some people think they should write about opinions, but most academic writing doesn't really work

---

* According to some scholars, Martin Luther (the sixteenth-century priest who started the Protestant Reformation) did not actually say this, but it's widely attributed to him, and it looks good at the beginning of a chapter on "stance."

this way. If you write one thousand words about why people who disagree with you are wrong and stupid, you'll alienate your readers, and you won't look like a sophisticated thinker or writer.

Instead, I think a better way to think about responding is to call it a "stance." I ask questions like this: Where do you stand in relation to the author? What is your position relative to the original text?

You'll notice that this is a metaphor that uses the concept of physical space to explain how you feel about an idea – imagine yourself at a party or something, and you're listening to somebody talk passionately about something they have a lot to say about. If you find what they're saying compelling, you might want to move closer to them. If you find what they're saying wrong or repulsive, you might want to get as far away from them as you can. And there are ways to do that with words.

In his article "The Rhetorical Stance," scholar Wayne Booth defines *stance* as the balance between three things:

- "the available arguments about the subject itself"

- the audience

- the voice of the speaker.

You can show your stance by doing the things I suggested in the last section – being explicit about where you agree or disagree, and critiquing the way the author makes their points. You can also do it with the language you use, especially in the following ways:

- Vary the verbs of attribution you use. Writing "Smith *implies* X" is tentative and suggests your stance is maybe farther away from the writer. Writing "Smith *clearly shows* X" is more certain and suggests you align yourself with the author.

- Use adjectives, adverbs, or modal verbs (like *might, could, may,* and so on) that signal various degrees of agreement or certainty when you attribute things to the author. The chart below has some examples of how you can do this, but there are many more possibilities.

Language	Stance relative to author
Smith unconvincingly attempts to show ...	Very far away
Smith seems to suggest ...	Pretty far away
Smith suggests ...	Not all that close, but almost neutral
Smith states ...	Neutral
Smith clearly shows ...	Pretty close
Smith unequivocally proves ...	Very close

 TL;DR: You can show your agreement or disagreement with texts not only by just telling your reader what you think but also by using certain kinds of words to show whether you align yourself closely with the original writer or not.

Plagiarism

Any speaker is himself a respondent to a greater or lesser
degree. He is not, after all, the first speaker, the one who
disturbs the eternal silence of the universe.

—M.M. Bakhtin, *Speech Genres and Other Late Essays*

Why We Acknowledge Other People's Words

People talk about plagiarism a lot at universities, and
it's important to understand and be careful about it. The
problem is, not everybody agrees on what plagiarism is.

There are some things we can all agree on: you
shouldn't pay people to write papers for you, or copy your
friend's paper, or have AI software write your paper and
put your name on it. If you turn in a paper with your name
on it but you did 0 percent of the writing, this is – well, it's
bad. Some people even think of it as stealing. (The Latin
word *plagarius* means "kidnapper" – using other people's
words without attribution is apparently as bad as stealing
a child!)

You can get in a lot of trouble if you do this sort of thing.
Some countries have passed laws against companies that

advertise "paper-writing services" to university students, and even if these services are not currently illegal where you live, it's almost certainly against your university's policy to pay someone to do your assignments.

That doesn't mean you can never get help with your writing. There are some grey areas. For example, it's totally fine to get someone's help editing your grammar and spelling, as long as they're not completely rewriting your paper. In some cases, you'll be encouraged to collaborate with others on some parts of a piece of writing. (My university does have a policy against the "unauthorized" use of an editor, but as ever, this usually depends on the individual course or instructor.) See the section "Feedback" for more about this.

So there are usually two different things people mean when they talk about plagiarism. The first is the obvious cheating-style situation in which the writer did not do most of the actual writing. The second, which is more common and somewhat harder to avoid, is the problem of not sufficiently explaining where ideas or words come from. (This is one reason we use citation styles like MLA and APA, which we'll talk about in a bit.)

But where *do* ideas come from? I'm tempted to quote another one of my favourite dorky nineties movies, *Empire Records,* where a character says, "Who knows where thoughts come from? They just appear!" Surely we don't have to explain how we know every single thing we know and cite a credible expert source on literally every fact we ever mention. Like, do you need to say, "According to an article in the *Guardian* newspaper, Queen Elizabeth II was the queen of England"? Do you need to cite a biology text-book when you tell your readers that bananas are a fruit?*

No, you don't have to provide citations for these things. Some ideas are so well-known they're considered "common knowledge." In fact, don't worry too much about having to provide a reference or a citation for things that you already had in your head before you started doing the readings you did for your class or assignment. And in some science disciplines, it's *important* to use the same language as other texts, like if you're replicating an experi-ment and you need to write out the exact name of a chem-ical compound or a procedure you followed. These aren't always cited.

The problem usually comes when you try to offer a summary or a close paraphrase of a text to make a new point. If you're not careful, your voice can start to blend with the voice of the original author, and it might look like you're claiming that you're the one who said or thought something that another writer said or thought.

You probably don't mean to "steal" words or ideas, but a general rule to remember is this: if it wasn't already

---

* I don't know why you'd be saying this – maybe you're writing a paper about the history of the banana import-export business.

rattling around in your head before you read the text, you need to attribute and probably cite that information. And as mentioned in the "Paraphrasing" section, if you find yourself using more than a few words in a row that are identical to the original text, you're going to need to quote or cite that too.

 TL;DR: Not everyone has the same understanding of what *plagiarism* means, but when you're writing in an academic setting, it's really important to explain that you read about an idea in another text.

Citations

How to Acknowledge Other People's Words

In academia, we use citation styles for the same reason we care about plagiarism: it's really important to clearly explain where words and ideas come from, and these styles are systematic and widely accepted ways to do that. Citations are like a trail back to the original source that the reader can follow if they want to. Human knowledge, all the way from the ancient philosopher to you, the twenty-first-century student, has a genealogy, and being clear about how it works is beneficial to you as a student and a writer, and to your professor as a teacher, and to any other readers, real or imagined, who might read your paper. Citation styles are one major way we do this.

There are many different styles in different fields, but two big ones you'll almost definitely come across in university are MLA (the Modern Language Association, mostly used in the humanities) and APA (the American Psychological Association, mostly used in the social sciences). If you know MLA from high school, APA will feel weird to you, but they're both fine – just different. Chicago style is also fairly common in some fields.

The two main things you should know about are

- *in-text citations:* found in the body of your paper
- *references:* the full information about the resource you used, found at the end of the paper in a list.

Here's what you need to know.

How to Use In-Text Citations, and Where to Look for Help If You Forget How

For APA style, you need to remember three things:

- author's last name
- year of publication
- page number.

An APA in-text citation looks something like this, although you can mix and match what goes in the parentheses and what goes in the actual sentence:

He later explains that "anyone who disagrees with you is a big dumb idiot" (Heng Hartse, 2022, p. 56).

For MLA style, generally you just need

- author's last name
- page number.

Also, MLA does not use "p." to introduce the page number, and it doesn't put a comma between the name and the number, both of which are different from APA. An MLA citation looks something like this:

He later explains that "anyone who disagrees with you is a big dumb idiot" (Heng Hartse 56).

Notice that for both APA and MLA, the period at the end of the sentence comes after the parenthesis. This can look weird if you're not used to it, but it's correct!

In Chicago style, in-text citations have the author's last name and the date, but also a comma before the page number, and no "p." in front of it. Kind of like a mix of MLA and APA:

He later explains that "anyone who disagrees with you is a big dumb idiot" (Heng Hartse 2022, 56).

If you forget how to do this or encounter a unique situation, I suggest searching for "APA style guide" or "MLA style guide," and so on, on the internet. Most organizations that have citation styles have their own websites that give advice on unique situations. You can also buy paper or electronic copies of the official style manuals, which I highly recommend because they're the most comprehensive guides, but if you'd rather not buy one, university libraries often have good free, short guides to the most common situations you'll face with APA and MLA style.

How to Figure Out How to Copy Automatically Formatted References

I really don't think you need to learn how to write references from scratch anymore. There are many ways to do this automatically, and they've gotten much better in recent years. You can look up how to correctly put an edited book or journal article or podcast in your list of sources (placed at the end of your paper – what APA and Chicago call "References" and MLA calls "Works Cited"), but honestly, most of the time, you don't have to look it up and type it all out yourself.

Instead, all you have to do is find the place on whatever library database or academic search engine you're using that will give you an automatic citation. In recent years, the most common symbol for automatically generated references has become a little box with quotation marks inside it, or just the word *Cite*. This will be a small button or link near the basic information about the article. Find this, click it, then copy the reference (in whatever style) and paste it into your References or Works Cited. This list should be in alphabetical order by the author's last name.

You may find there are errors with the automatic citations from time to time; specifically, the way they capitalize (or don't capitalize) the titles of books or articles can differ from what the style guide calls for. Here's a quick rule to remember.

APA → **Sentence case**
MLA and Chicago → **Headline or title case**

APA. Titles of articles and books are in what is called "sentence case," meaning you only capitalize the first letter of the title, any proper nouns in the title, and the first letter after a colon or other punctuation mark. However, the titles of academic journals are in what is called "title case," meaning that every word except for prepositions (like *of* or *in*) and articles (like *a* or *the*) is capitalized. Here's a journal article in APA style:

Drake, C. A. (1941). Why students cheat. *Journal of Higher Education, 12*(8), 418–20.

MLA. Unlike in APA style, titles of everything in MLA style are in what is called "headline or title case." Here's the same example:

Drake, Charles A. "Why Students Cheat." *Journal of Higher Education* vol. 12, no. 8 (1941), pp. 418–20.

Chicago. This style is pretty similar to MLA style, with a few variations.

Drake, Charles A. "Why Students Cheat." *Journal of Higher Education* 12, no. 8 (1941): 418–20.

You'll notice each style has different ways of showing you the volume and issue number of journals: "*12*(8)" in APA, "vol. 12, no. 8" in MLA, and "12, no. 8" in Chicago all mean "volume 12, issue 8" of the journal. I don't think you need to know a whole lot about this unless you plan to go to graduate school, but don't worry – the information is out there if you need it, and somewhere on your campus right now there's a reference librarian who can't wait to help you figure it out if you want.

TL;DR: MLA, APA, and Chicago style citations are ways we show where the stuff we're writing about comes from. They're different, and you can learn more from the internet about whichever one you're using. Automatic citations are your friend, but they're not always right.

THREE

Writing "The Paper"

What "The Paper" Is

Papers are chances to take care of
little pieces of your soul.

—Luke Reinsma, during a class I took from him

What's a "paper" in university? It depends (surprise!) on what your professor says, what class you're in, and what the assignment is.

If you're in a first-year writing or composition course, you'll probably be assigned what is often called a "research paper," or what we called a "paper from sources" in the "Genre" section of this book. In its most basic form, this is a piece of writing that will make a point about some issue related to the course. Your professor may give you a "topic" (this is a word I don't like, which I'll explain later), or you might have to choose your own.

This may feel, like many first-year writing assignments, a bit fake. In real life, you're almost never put in a situation where your boss at work, or whoever, says, "Write something!" And you ask, "What should I write?" And they say, "I don't care. Just make an argument about whether drugs should be legalized, or climate change, or something!"

If this is how you felt when you got your "paper" assignment, I'm sorry. When I was in college, I had a professor who told us that writing a paper was a chance to take care of a little piece of your soul, which is something I really liked. He was giving us the freedom to pursue something that might matter to us, to approach a problem that bothered us, to learn about something we wanted to learn more about. Ideally, any writing assignment will at least have some part of that in it.

So, here's how a paper – which from now on I will refer to in title case, as The Paper, to make it look more important – usually emerges:

1 You're studying a certain subject or academic discipline, or have at least done some readings about a certain issue or problem, in one of your courses.

2 You're given an assignment to write a longish text related to that subject or discipline or issue or problem. (The definition of *longish* varies. The Paper is usually more than two or three pages. In some courses, it may be around four or five pages, or 1,000 to 2,000 words; in others, especially in your upper-year courses, you may get up into the eight- or ten- or fifteen-page territory.) This assignment usually comes in the second half of a course and is usually one of the final assignments you turn in, often for a large chunk of your grade.

3   Usually for this assignment, you need to do more reading about the specific thing you're writing about. Your professor might have a handful of readings you're meant to draw from; more often, you may have to find these on your own.

4   You need to figure out how to write about the thing in a way that expresses a position or stance or argument (that is, your "original" idea, in some way) by using or drawing on the texts you read in step no. 3 or no. 1 or both.

5   You need to find a way to make The Paper coherent and cohesive – one whole thing rather than a lot of little unrelated parts or a list of semi-related points or ideas.

Numbers 1 and 2 are pretty simple, and the course you're in will usually prepare you for them well. Numbers 3, 4, and 5 are a bit more complicated. We'll review them in the coming sections.

 TL;DR: In a lot of classes, you have to write a long paper that uses academic articles, books, or book chapters as sources to make a somewhat original point about something related to the class.

Structure

Tell 'em what you're gonna tell them. Tell 'em.
Tell 'em what you told 'em.

—Mr. Ulmen, my Grade 7 English teacher
(and probably thousands of teachers throughout history)

Make the Paper Do What You Say It's Going to Do

We've already talked about genre, and this is the part of the book where I should tell you about some different genres or types of The Paper. I'm not sure I really want to do this, however. Usually, a book like this would list different types of papers you could write, with different structures:

- *argumentation:* trying to prove a point or persuade the reader that something is true

- *comparison:* showing how two things are alike or different

- *cause and effect:* explaining the cause(s) of something

- *problem and solution:* proposing and evaluating various solutions to a particular problem

- *narrative:* telling a story about something
- *exposition:* explaining or offering information about some phenomenon.

These can be helpful ways to think about different purposes your paper might have, but I'm not going to go into detail about each of them, for a few reasons.

First, The Paper is not a stable enough genre for me to be able to break it down into all these different categories and tell you how to write each one. People who teach writing classes, or classes that involve writing a paper, have many different opinions about how to write The Paper and what it should include.

For example, I don't really think cause and effect is a real genre; I think it's actually just an argumentative paper, because the purpose of a cause-and-effect paper is to persuade a reader that Thing B has various causes: X, Y, and Z. In a way, they're all just argumentative papers, because usually the purpose of The Paper is to make a point about something that the reader might not have known or believed or considered before.

But even good argumentative papers shouldn't really be argumentative in the "let's fight with words" way that our culture, especially on the internet, seems to demand.

I think we would all be better writers, and just better people, if we could tone down what the rhetoric scholar Robert Connors (and others) calls "agonistic" writing –

that kind of hardcore "debate" style that looks to score points and win arguments by crushing the loser with a deadly blow of reasoning. We could instead embrace what he (and others) call the "irenic" style, one that attempts to do its persuasion by means of consensus-building and seeking peace. But maybe that's just me.

My other reasons for not giving you cheat sheets for these different genres or structures is that they're overly simplistic. I don't think I've ever really seen a good academic paper I would categorize as only argumentative, or only comparative, and so on.

Honestly, I still believe the basic structure of most academic papers is as simple as my Grade 7 English teacher, Mr. Ulmen, taught us:

1 Tell 'em what you're gonna tell 'em.

2 Tell 'em.

3 Tell 'em what you told 'em.

I often tell students that they can organize their papers however they want, as long as they have declared a clear purpose, and the paper makes good on the declared purpose. I think of this as the paper following its own "internal logic."

What does that mean? Of course, the things you write about should all be related to the thesis statement, and we'll talk more about this soon. But on an even more surface level, I really think you should come out and declare things clearly and obviously. You don't have to say it exactly this way, but I honestly think papers should say something like this:

My purpose in writing this paper is to explain why [Thing X] has been misunderstood by people who believe [Idea Y], and how current research in [Discipline C] clearly shows that [Thing Y is wrong and Idea Z makes more sense]. First, I'll explain the history of [Thing X] and how historical and cultural influences have made it the way it is. Then I'll explore the debates and disagreements between [people who believe Idea Y and people who believe Idea Z]. I'll also show how [Idea Z] can help us solve [Problems A and B with Thing X] and gives us hopeful new ideas for how to deal with [Thing X] in the future, even as [Problems A and B, and even possible New Problems D and E] exist.

I just made this structure up. You may not want to write about something that is misunderstood, or its history, or the other things I wrote. And, of course, all the stuff with letters would be real things in a real paper. But what I want to draw your attention to here is laying out all your cards on the table for the reader – give a clear map or blueprint or plan of what you plan to do in the paper and make sure you go on to follow it. We'll talk more about this later.

⚡ **TL;DR:** The Paper can have many different purposes and structures, but as long as you explain what you're going to do and actually follow through on it, you should be OK.

Creating an Outline (If You Want To)

You don't always *need* to write an outline, but sometimes your professor will ask you to. Use this as an opportunity to do some work that will help you organize your thoughts and help your instructor know what you plan to write about so they can offer you some advice.

If you *do* do an outline, you need to have done a lot of reading, because the outline needs to offer some idea of both the content and structure of your paper.

In terms of content, it's important to have some idea of what you want to say, rather than just an outline that says, "First, I'll introduce something, then make a point about it, then make another point about it, and then conclude the paper." That doesn't really help you plan your paper, or help your prof help you.

There are a lot of ways to structure a paper, and you shouldn't feel tied to a specific one. Many people are used to Intro | Three-Paragraph Body | Conclusion, which can be OK, but it is equally fine to have just two body paragraphs for a short paper, or seven or ten or more for a longer paper. The important thing is that every part of The Paper needs to clearly feel like it's related to the stated purpose of The Paper, which is usually the thesis statement.

Don't worry about making your outline perfect, and don't feel you absolutely must stick to it. If something you planned to write about in your outline isn't working, you can abandon it once you start writing.

 TL;DR: An outline is a map of your paper, and it can help you make sure that everything in the paper fits together well. The more detailed it is, the more it will help.

Topic

> [Students] have to invent the university by assembling and mimicking its language, finding some compromise between idiosyncrasy, a personal history, and the requirements of convention, the history of a discipline.
>
> —Donald Bartholomae, "Inventing the University"

Moving from a Topic to a Question

In some guides to academic writing, they call the first stage of the writing process – the part where you figure out what to write about – "invention."

This term has never quite made sense to me, because when you're starting university, you usually don't have much freedom to just *invent* something to write about out of thin air. More often than not, your instructor will have some guidelines regarding what it is you're meant to write about.

A lot of people call this your "topic," but I also don't think this term is useful.

The main reason I don't like *topics* is that this term encourages us to oversimplify things. People tend to talk about topics in extremely broad and nonspecific language.

So if your topic is, I don't know, climate change, and you're not sure where to begin, you'll type *climate change* into a search engine or database and get 1,620,000,000 results and still have no idea where to begin. Plus, what can you learn or discover or explain about the generic topic of climate change that can't be done in a five-minute skim of a Wikipedia page? "The climate is changing because of pollution, which is bad." Ten words. Now what?

Also, when you start searching for resources, you might get a bunch of results from different perspectives. If your topic is global pandemics (something pretty much everyone in the world was interested in when I started writing this book, and something we'll all probably be interested in for years to come) and you type some relevant terms into an academic database, you might find information from medical researchers, virologists, epidemiologists, sociologists, psychologists, and historians. Do you need all of these perspectives? They're definitely all valuable in their own way, but it's also possible that trying to cram them all into a paper will result in something confusing and incoherent, and you might end up with too many different conversations with too many different audiences. Plus, your history professor might not think you need to cite the virologists, and your biology professor might not think you need to cite the historians.

So the problem with thinking about topics is that topics can be vague, confusing, and, often, just bland and boring.

Instead, try to think of your paper as addressing a *problem* or a *question* that you can answer in the scope of a few (or however many) pages.

If you find that you have to start with a big topic, try to focus on a small part of it, and find an interesting question you can ask about that small part. Narrow and narrow and narrow down your idea for a paper. Use your own experience, interests, and desires to hone in on a tiny little piece of a bigger issue.

Let's look at an example of narrowing:

Big, boring, generic topic: **language and society**
⚡ It's unlikely you'll get a topic *this* broad on an assignment, but I had to pick one I know something about.

Narrower: **the use of Chinese in North America**
⚡ This is already way better. We have a pretty good idea of what we're focusing on now, although there are still a lot of different angles one could take: Is this going to be a paper about the teaching of Chinese at American schools and colleges? Or bilingualism in the Chinese Canadian community? Or the linguistic landscape of airports that use English, Chinese, French, and other languages on signs? Those are just a few possibilities. We need to keep narrowing.

Narrower still: bilingual Chinese-English education programs in western Canada

⚡ OK, we're getting pretty specific now, and this is starting to sound interesting. Still, depending on what course this paper is for, there are still some different approaches we might take. Do you want to talk about teaching methods? Do you want to say something about equity and access to language education for people from different backgrounds? Do you want to compare historical influences on British Columbia's and Alberta's education systems?

Now let's turn the narrower topic into an answerable question. Not all of these are going to be great – I'm just throwing out ideas at this point.

- What is the history of bilingual education in British Columbia, and how does Chinese fit into it?

- What teaching methods do bilingual kindergarten teachers use in Canada?

- How has Alberta handled the demand for Chinese and other languages in its bilingual education programs?

- How are French-language education and Chinese-language education different and/or similar in British Columbia?

I don't know how to find the answers to these questions yet. But if I *have* a question, I'm ready to start trying to figure out how I can answer it.

 TL;DR: Try not to start with a big, broad, generic "topic" for your paper but think instead of a problem you'd like to solve or a question you'd like to answer.

Sources

Writing from sources is what we do in university.

—Doug Brent, "The Research Paper
and Why We Should Still Care"

At some point during the writing of The Paper, you'll prob-ably need to do your own digging for sources.

As usual, your first course of action should be checking the parameters of the assignment. Reread the directions carefully, and if you're still not clear, ask a classmate, a TA, or writing centre tutor, or someone you trust who's an aca-demic "insider" – that is, someone who knows the game of writing for university and ideally knows something about the area you're writing in. In some cases, your prof might have parameters like telling you to only use certain jour-nals, or certain databases, when you look for sources.

Tips on Finding Sources

There are two places you might look: your university's library website and Google Scholar. They both work OK, but Google Scholar is likely to be more familiar to you at first. However, Google changed its motto from "Don't Be Evil" to something else in 2015, which should tell you something. And I assume your university library is not a giant for-profit corporation whose main goal is collecting personal information about you in order to sell advertising, but that's not the point.

Here's the problem you're going to run into, Google or no Google: TOO MUCH INFORMATION. Seriously. Scholarly publishing has exploded in the last twenty or thirty years, and no one can keep up with all the published research in any field anymore. It's simply not possible to read even a tiny fraction of what is published in any area in any given year. The best most of us can do is to read important foundational texts in our fields and to keep up with some of the best-known and most well-respected academic journals that cover our disciplines, and even that is not easy.

To make matters worse, there has also been an explosion of poor-quality academic research. It's too complicated to explain the reasons why here, but there are thousands of poorly written, poorly argued, and inaccurate academic articles available in any keyword search you might be interested in, and it can be hard to spot them. (More on this later.)

What should you do when faced with this firehose of information? Here are some rules that are not always 100 percent accurate but should help:

- *Make sure your sources are recent, usually within the last ten or twenty years.* It's different if your assignment requires you to do historical or archival research, of course, and in some cases, you'll need to read older texts in order to understand historical perspectives on the phenomena you're studying, but it's important to know what the important issues are in the area *currently.*

- *Make sure most of your sources are academic.* Hot tip: If you're going to Google, use Google Scholar (scholar.google.com) not regular Google (google.com) – always! What makes a source "academic"? According to Wikipedia, an academic publication is one "in which scholarship relating to a particular academic discipline is published." Usually, these are academic journals or books, but sometimes they can be things like preprint repositories, which are websites that host papers written by researchers before they're published in academic journals (a site called arXiv is a popular example of this). Some nonacademic sources from credible institutions are often OK: the *New York Times* or a university-affiliated website or a well-known think tank would be all right, as long as they are balanced out by other academic sources. A random teenager's TikTok account would not be a good source to use in a research paper.

- *Use a lot of different combinations of keywords in your searches.* Your first idea for a search term might not be the word experts in that area use. *Cheating* is one way to talk about something, but *academic dishonesty* or *academic misconduct* or *academic integrity* might get you further. Try to figure out what the people who research this thing call it. Oh, and if your keywords are a phrase, be sure to put them all inside quotation marks.

- *Read titles and skim abstracts and reference lists.* Find which articles look interesting or relevant from their titles, then read their abstracts to see if they fit what you're looking for. Read *a lot* of abstracts. Read, like, fifteen or twenty, even if you're only looking for three or four good sources. Skim the reference lists of articles that you like, and look up a few articles with interesting titles. Repeat this until you've got as many good-quality articles as you can handle reading, or at least skimming.

- *Make sure the journals you're looking at are part of the conversation your professor wants you to be learning about.* This can be hard to do. If you're in an education course that takes a more qualitative, social approach to student well-being, you might not want to look for many articles that take a more quantitative, "hard numbers" approach to student success. In addition, you need to watch out for journals that are outside the mainstream academic conversation your professor is hoping to teach you about. This is such a tricky thing to navigate that the next section is going to deal with it in more detail.

 TL;DR: Try to find a lot of high-quality, recent journal articles that are relevant to the thing you're writing about.

Tips on Making Sure Your Sources Are Credible

Credibility just means whether a source can be believed or trusted – in this case, in an academic context. There are two problems you might run into when it comes to credibility:

- finding sources that seem relevant to what you want to write about but that are not appropriate for an academic paper

- finding sources that seem relevant to what you want to talk about and seem to be from legitimate academic publishers but are actually from low-quality or scam publications.

The first one is simpler to talk about. For a few reasons, there are some kinds of sources that aren't used in academic writing. For example, a tabloid newspaper like the

Daily Mail has a bad reputation for publishing sensational celebrity gossip that may or may not be true. Similarly, it usually isn't OK to use a random person's blog, personal website, or social media account as a source to prove a point or as evidence that something you're writing about is true. Even more trustworthy media sources like newspapers, magazines, or news websites aren't usually the main sources used in academic writing, though they certainly can be used in some disciplines. Why is this?

In the academic world, the currency of credibility is something we call "peer review." It isn't perfect, but it helps to assure the quality and trustworthiness of the knowledge produced by research. This is how the peer review process works:

1 A researcher engages in a project according to the standards of their discipline (we get trained on how to do this, often for years).

2 They write about what they learned in their project.

3 They submit the article or book they wrote to an academic journal or book publisher.

4 The publisher sends the article or book out to two, three, or four respected scholars who work in the same field as the researcher – almost always without the researcher's name on it, so they can judge it fairly – and those people write reviews. They evaluate things

like whether the research methods were followed correctly, whether the theory the researcher used makes sense, whether the conclusions they came to make sense, and whether the claims they make about the thing they studied are warranted.

This process isn't always 100 percent perfect. Every once in a while, someone submits a fake article as a joke, and it gets published, and every once in a while, there are big disagreements among scholars about whether a paper was really good enough to be published. But the process goes a long way in making sure that the research published is done well, and in good faith, and can be trusted. Peer-reviewed papers and books written by scholars who work at well-known, respected universities throughout the world tend to be the types of conversations your own professors are involved in, and they tend to produce the type of knowledge that they hope you'll learn.

The reason I keep saying "Google Scholar, not regular Google" is that if you use regular Google, you'll get a ton of resources that look relevant and useful but are not peer reviewed and are generally not used by specialists, researchers, and scholars in the area you're learning about. This doesn't mean that the information in those sources is always bad (sometimes it is, though!). It just means it's not part of that academic conversation we talked about.

There's also another, newer problem with credibility, which is that in the last ten years or so there are hundreds and hundreds of new academic journals that *aren't* credible, for a few reasons:

- Some journals exploit writers, charging high fees to scholars who are desperate to publish their work.

- Some of those journals don't have good peer review practices and publish almost anything, even if it's total garbage.

- Some of those journals misrepresent their location, who their editors are, and other such things in order to seem more "international" than they really are.

- Some newer journals, even if they're more credible and are not attempting to just make money off writers, have lower standards than others and might publish work that is poorly written or poorly researched.

I don't have a foolproof solution about how to tell a scam journal from a good journal. My suggestions would be this. If an article has a lot of citations, chances are it's worth at least looking at. You can see this on Google Scholar underneath the info about the article on the search page – it will say "cited by 4" or "cited by 853," etc. But don't always accept an article's credibility at face value. If something seems "off," like the website is poorly designed or there are a lot of language mistakes in the article, it might not be trustworthy. When in doubt, ask an academic "insider" for some advice.

 TL;DR: Peer-reviewed academic texts are mainly what you should use for sources. However, there are some low-quality academic articles out there, so you've got to be careful.

How to Use Sources Once You've Found Them

We've already talked about how to paraphrase and quote other texts, but what does it actually mean to "use" the three or four or fifteen (or whatever) sources you've found and have been reading for your paper?

Sometimes it's easier to say what *not* to do. There are two extremes that people tend to fall into.

Quote mining. This is where you skim through a reading until you find a sentence or phrase that looks like it supports whatever you already believe, and you pluck it out and drop it into your paper without really explaining it. Then you do this again with four or five more sources. You're left with a paper that's really just a bunch of stuff you made up without thinking too much, and without much real support aside from a few awkwardly shoved-in quotes.

Accidentally writing a literature review. This is where you write a bunch of summaries of academic texts when the assignment *isn't* a literature review. (A literature review, which is a comprehensive series of summaries of relevant articles about a given subject, is usually more of an upper-year or grad school assignment.) The problem here is that your paper is no longer thesis-driven. It becomes a list of summaries of every reading you did but with an introduction and a conclusion slapped on either end. Unlike the quote-mining paper, the accidental literature review has almost *none* of your own ideas in it.

Instead of falling into these extremes, a paper that uses its sources well will look like the product of an encounter between you and the texts you've read. You come to a topic (or idea or problem) with an interest in it and some ideas about what you might want to say, but you allow the texts you read to shape your understanding, and you enter into a kind of conversation with them – a conversation guided by a purpose you choose, even though it may change as you write. Think of the process looking this way:

1 You've got an initial idea of what you want to write about, because you've already done the course readings and taken notes on them, and you've got a problem or question or even something resembling a thesis statement.

2 You find some more relevant sources and read them while taking notes.

3 You think about what you read and allow it to help you edit or change your thesis statement.

4 You start writing about the thing you want to say, and as you explain and expand on your points, you summarize and paraphrase parts of the sources that add something meaningful to your point.

5 As you write, you allow the stuff in the readings to influence and change your main points, arguments, and ideas. Maybe you start thinking one thing and realize it's more complicated or different than you thought, so your paper changes as a result. This is a good thing – in fact, it's the whole point. In the process of reading and writing, you're also learning and thinking.

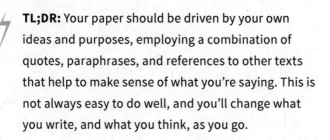

TL;DR: Your paper should be driven by your own ideas and purposes, employing a combination of quotes, paraphrases, and references to other texts that help to make sense of what you're saying. This is not always easy to do well, and you'll change what you write, and what you think, as you go.

Thesis Statements

The defining characteristics of a high quality thesis
statement seem arbitrary and subjective.

—Daniel Chang, "What's within a Thesis Statement?"

Explaining Your Point in One Sentence

Thesis statements are another one of those things that
everyone thinks are important but that people have
trouble defining. Usually, a thesis statement is the final
sentence of The Paper's introduction, and it expresses the
main focus of the paper as a whole.

The Paper is almost always thesis-driven, meaning that
it has a clearly defined main purpose, something it's trying
to do. (Well, something *you,* the writer, are trying to do.)

As we've discussed, usually that thing is referred to as
"making an argument" or "proving a point" or otherwise
persuading a reader about something. Remember, this
doesn't have to be a capital-A argument of the "I'm right,
and you're stupid" variety. Often, the thesis is more complex than a simple black-or-white argument.

The thesis statement can be the outcome of the narrowing process I described in the "Topic" section. Let's try that again, but instead of coming up with a question, let's try to answer it by creating a thesis statement. We will start with an overly simple statement, using one of my favourite issues, academic integrity. I'm going to try to write a series of thesis statements starting with general, vague, bad ones and gradually make them better using my own interests and what I've learned by skimming relevant readings.

BAD **Academic integrity is important.**
⚡ Too general.

STILL BAD **Academic integrity is important for universities today.**
⚡ Still not good but at least it provides some context.

NOT GREAT **Universities should not harshly punish students who violate academic integrity.**
⚡ At least it shows a strong position on the issue.

BETTER **Universities should be more specific about how they define academic integrity violations.**
⚡ Getting more specific now.

EVEN BETTER **University policies need to more clearly define plagiarism so students are not unfairly punished for making mistakes.**

⚡ Still uses somewhat generic language.

REALLY GOOD **Universities need clearer policies about how plagiarism is defined, and they need to take a teaching-oriented approach to dealing with cases of plagiarism rather than a punishment-oriented approach. Most plagiarism cases are the result of ignorance of the norms of academic communication rather than intentionally deceptive violations of the rules.**

⚡ Clear context, stance, reasoning, and specificity.

You don't have to know exactly what your thesis statement is when you start writing, but doing something like this at the beginning of the process will help. You will probably change it as you continue to read and write, and that's OK.

 TL;DR: The thesis statement comes at the end of your first paragraph (that is, the introduction) and is a single sentence that says what your paper is about as clearly as possible.

Introductions

I don't know where to begin.

—Death Cab for Cutie, "No Room in Frame"

How to Begin

The introduction is the first paragraph of The Paper, and it offers a general-to-specific explanation of the things you're going to be writing about. Usually, your introduction should function like an upside-down triangle, with the wide part at the top representing general information about the broad domain or topic the paper will touch on, and the point at the bottom representing the specific area of your focus. Here's a generic version of what it could look like. (Bonus: the whole intro looks like a big arrow pointing to the rest of your paper, which is kind of what it is!)

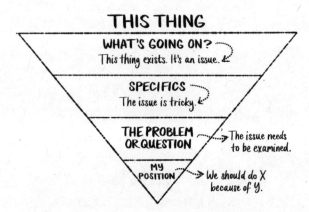

There are other ways to do it, but you can't go wrong with this. For the fat part of the triangle at the top, though, don't start with a dictionary definition. Professors hate that.

The last part of the introduction paragraph should usually include the thesis statement and/or a brief sketch of the structure of the paper – like a blueprint or a map of what the reader can expect.

As mentioned earlier, I really believe this second point is the most important part of the paper. If this sketch is wrong, the whole paper will seem like it didn't do what it was supposed to. It's got to actually match what comes in the rest of the paper. If it doesn't, you'll have to either change this part or change the rest of the paper.

 TL;DR: Move from general to specific in an introduction and end with a thesis statement and a map of where the paper is going to go.

Paragraphs

Putting Together Sentences

The paragraphs in the middle of The Paper are usually called "body paragraphs." I don't know why.

A paragraph is just a bunch of sentences about a particular thing, put together. It doesn't really matter how long a paragraph is, but in an academic paper, if you're under about three sentences, they usually look too short, and if you're over about ten, they look too long. (A paragraph that is longer than a page is almost never a good idea. It's too easy for a reader to get lost without the visual cues of indentation when a new idea begins.) The sentences in a paragraph should be related in some way; the sentence at the beginning of the paragraph usually sums up the basic idea of the paragraph – this is called the "topic sentence." It helps to think of the topic sentence as a mini-thesis statement, since it should relate back to your overall thesis statement in some way.

Paragraphs are useful for signalling to your reader where you're going with your ideas. Breaking up text into visually readable chunks is even more important to readers today than, say, thirty years ago. In fact, the expression

TL;DR (remember?) is most often used in order to summarize giant paragraphs of text no one wants to read on the internet.

If we had to come up with a formula for where paragraph breaks should go, it would be something like this:

There have already been a lot of sentences in this paragraph

+

it looks like a new idea of some kind is starting now

=

paragraph break.

It depends on your prof's guidelines, but usually you'll want to create paragraphs by indenting and *not* putting a line space between paragraphs. And don't do both; it looks weird.

Use the "tab" key on your computer keyboard to indent and make a paragraph break. Do not create indentations by hitting the space bar a bunch of times. It'll really mess everything up.

You might have written five-paragraph essays in high school, but it doesn't matter how many body paragraphs there are in a paper. There could be two or three or seven or eighteen depending on the requirements of the assignment and the purpose of the paper. It just matters that your paragraphs make points that are directly related to the paper's overall purpose as laid out in the thesis statement. Some people say you need to have a separate paragraph that introduces a "counterargument," but if you're writing in such a way that you're always in "conversation" with your sources, I don't think this is necessary (unless your instructor has really specific requirements).

 TL;DR: Paragraphs are collections of related sentences and shouldn't be too long. You can have as many as you want as long as they're clearly related to the paper's overall purpose.

Conclusions

How to End

Conclusions aren't easy to write. Somehow it seems hard to sum up everything you've said so far in a meaningful way without repeating yourself or seeming overly self-important. I hate writing conclusions so much that I usually don't even label anything "conclusion" when I write an academic article, and I hope no one notices. But a piece of writing has to end somewhere.

Usually, a conclusion is a paragraph (or several paragraphs, in a longer paper) that does two things.

Summarize. A conclusion reminds readers about what you just said in the paper. It can be hard to do this without repeating yourself, but if you use some strategies that we talk about in the sections on paraphrasing and cohesion, you should be able to get through this with just a bit of language reuse. The goal is to re-emphasize your main points and purpose.

Synthesize. A conclusion makes it all come to some new, final, emerging insight. (Don't introduce brand new evidence or examples or supporting information, though.) It's like the flower that grows out of the dirt of the paper, or, to continue the plant metaphor, the garden that grows from the soil of the rest of the paper. It's made of the same stuff, but it emerges as something new. You might also think of synthesis sentences as answering questions like these:

- So what?

- Who cares?

- What should happen next, given [everything I said in this paper]?

- Given [everything I said in this paper], what is import-ant to know or do?

- What should people who just read this paper be think-ing about now?

You can think of the end of the paper as a kind of call to action. You don't have to be super dramatic about it, but try to show your readers why what you wrote might matter in the real world. It doesn't even have to be a real action – it can just be a suggestion for them to think more carefully about something.

Here are a few examples of conclusions I wrote when I was a student – I'll give you the last sentence or two of three papers. I'm not going to promise that they're perfect, but I got OK grades.

Augustine's *Confessions* do just what they set out to accomplish: we learn by Augustine's example. In his spiritual journey we can see more clearly our own.

⚡ I wrote this as a first-year undergraduate, and it seems OK. I can see how a reader might be intrigued about this and want to read the book.

For the sake of our students, a conversation must begin among ESL writing teachers, researchers, and administrators about how we understand the concept of culture and whether traditional understandings are adequate. We must begin to change. The world has.

⚡ This is the final section of my master's thesis. I'll be honest, it's pretty cringe. It's unnecessarily dramatic. Yet I do think it's doing something a conclusion should: giving one final push to the reader that says, "You should care about this!"

China remains one of the most important centres of language teaching and learning in the world, and the future will bring new innovations in the way foreign teachers are integrated into its massive project of English education.

⚡ I wrote this as a PhD student, and I think it's pretty good – it's a lot less dramatic than the above, and it seems like it would make readers interested in learning more about what's going to happen in the near future in this area.

 TL;DR: The conclusion should remind readers of your main points without repeating them exactly or introducing new information, and it should leave them with a sense of why what you said matters.

Flow

Coherence and Cohesion

When I ask people what good writing should do, they usually say it should "flow." When I ask them what *flow* means, they usually have no idea how to answer.

What they're really talking about are coherence and cohesion.

Coherence is how all the parts of a piece of writing fit together at the big-picture level. Does the intro match the body? Does each paragraph seem related to the thesis? Does the conclusion wrap everything up? And so on. This is easier to get right than cohesion because you can look at a paragraph and say to yourself, "Oh, I can see that this paragraph talks about something unrelated to what I said the paper was going to be about in the introduction. I better change it."

In most of my classes, I draw something that looks like this on the board (this looks better, though, because I asked a professional illustrator to draw it):

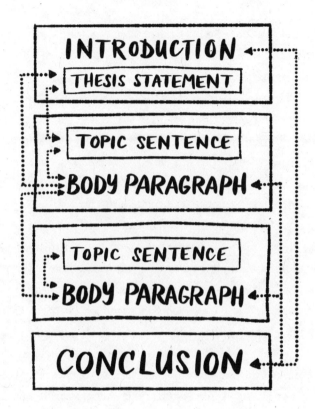

Notice that all of the arrows point in two directions. All of these things should in some way point to each other. The thesis should point toward each paragraph's topic sentence, which should point back to the thesis. Each topic sentence should prepare the reader for the rest of the paragraph; each sentence in a body paragraph should point back to its topic sentence. The conclusion should point back to the body and the thesis. And so on.

Cohesion is how well the parts hang together at the sentence and word level. This is probably what most people think of as flow.

There are two main ways to create cohesion.

The first way is to use a lot of words that refer to other words in your text and be clear about what they refer to. This way of flowing has to do with the *meanings of words.* Pronouns like *it, that,* and *this* will point your reader to other things in your text and make the flow stronger – *if* you're clear about what "this" and "that" are. (Usually, the closest noun or phrase that comes before one of these words is what it refers to.) You can also use synonyms to do this. (Like, if your paper is about academic dishonesty, you can use words like *academic misconduct, cheating, academic integrity,* and so on throughout the paper.)

The second way is to use more traditional conjunction or "connector" words and phrases. This might be what you think of as "transition" words. This way of flowing has to do with words that are more about the structure of sentences. You should learn a lot of these and learn the differences between them. They include conjunction words like *for, and, nor, but, or, yet, so* and phrases like *furthermore, nevertheless, anyway, instead, besides, as a result of, instead of, in addition to, therefore, on the contrary, as a result, in addition, because of,* and so on. There are a lot. Getting to know them and using a wide variety of them is important.

Another Note on Transitions

You can use obvious "transition words" at the beginning of paragraphs, and those will work OK. The really, really obvious ones sometimes feel tired and overused, though. I don't usually recommend starting each paragraph with "firstly," "secondly," "thirdly" and so on, and I don't usually think a conclusion should start with "In conclusion." It's not wrong to do this, but I always encourage people to use the actual content of what they're writing about to make transitions rather than relying on these types of words.

Let me give a quick example from one of the papers I quoted in the "Conclusions" section. It's the final sentence of one paragraph and the beginning of the next one:

Maley (1983) comments on other difficulties, like unrealistic expectations of both foreign teachers and their employers, isolation of foreign teachers, and lack of detailed information about foreign teachers' objectives.

The number of foreign English teachers in China continues to grow, yet the difficulties that Maley first noticed in the early eighties continue to be common for foreign teachers in China today.

Note that the paragraph doesn't start with an obvious transition word, but does repeat a number of words from the previous sentence – *foreign teachers, difficulties,* and

Maley (the scholar I quote in the previous paragraph). It also makes a shift in the time frame discussed – the first paragraph quotes a paper from 1983, and the new paragraph mentions that year, as well as things happening "today" – that is, now, when I was writing the paper. With little things like this, you can usually avoid overly relying on those classic (overused) transition words.

 TL;DR: Flow means coherence and cohesion, which are largely done by using words that point to other words in your text.

Making Changes

The only way I can get anything written at all is to write
really, really shitty first drafts.

—Anne Lamott, *Bird by Bird*

Rewriting and Editing

You should always assume that the first draft you pound
out is going to be, more or less, garbage.

Sorry. It's this way for everyone, even really good
writers.

I heard once that the word *draft* often has different a
meaning for students than professors:

- *Student:* A draft is not quite finished – maybe missing
  a body paragraph and a conclusion, no references, no
  in-text citations, some parts are just notes jotted down
  to yourself, some parts are cut-and-pasted excerpts
  from articles you read that you plan to paraphrase
  later. You're hoping to get some feedback about what
  to write next or just buy some time until you sit down
  to really finish.

- *Prof:* A draft is a complete, turned-in paper with references and citations, maybe already proofread once or twice by the student, that will eventually be significantly changed and rewritten, even though the student already worked really hard on it and it looks finished.

Whatever your draft looks like, *revision* (also known as *rewriting*) is one of the most important parts of writing The Paper. For most writers, this is where 50 to 70 percent of the actual stuff you see in the finished paper happens.

Hopefully, you'll get some good feedback from your professor or TA (or a friend or two, or someone in the writing centre, etc.), and then have enough time to put the paper away and not think about it for a few days, and then come back to it with fresh eyes (re-vision, literally!).

Even if your prof doesn't ask for a draft, I highly, highly, *highly,* HIGHLY recommend doing some version of what I said in the last paragraph. You should assume you'll make *many* major changes to your paper during the revision process. Maybe you'll remove or rearrange whole paragraphs, delete or add multiple sentences, rearrange huge chunks, make the introduction the conclusion and write a new introduction – whatever works.

Editing and Proofreading

Revising is different from what we call "editing" or "proofreading." (These things have official definitions used by professional editors, but we'll talk about the more general way these words are used in academic writing.) Revising is making radical changes to the content of the paper; it's basically the same thing as writing – just, you know, more of it.

What many people call editing or proofreading involves making the final finishing touches, where you make sure everything is working right – grammar, punctuation, citations, precise and correct word choices, formatting. You won't catch everything when you do this, but 95 percent of the time there will be obvious mistakes you didn't notice at first that you'll catch if you go over it one last time.

Some general tips for editing:

- Have someone else do it.

- Be aware of issues that challenge you (verb tenses? commas? subject-verb agreement?) and read the paper through once just paying attention to those specific issues.

- Once you're satisfied with the coherence, try reading backwards, sentence-by-sentence, to look for errors at the sentence level.

 TL;DR: Your paper probably will and should change a lot from the first draft to the last. It's best to write, put it aside for a bit, and then come back to rewrite. Be sure to check for errors (and/or have someone else do it) before you turn something in.

FOUR

Other Stuff You Should Know

Feedback

Where to Get Help

Writing shouldn't be lonely. I understand that you often need to pound out something quickly and turn it in on time for class, but ideally, if you're writing more than one draft of a paper, you'll have a chance to get more pairs of eyes on whatever you write. Below are some common sources of help you might choose. No matter which of these you use, it's important to let whoever is helping you know as much as they can about the assignment: show them a copy of the syllabus or the assignment rubric if your instructor has provided them.

Peer Feedback

Many instructors use peer feedback in writing classes. It can feel a bit weird to comment on your classmates' drafts, but it helps in three big ways:

- you get to see how other people are approaching the assignment

- you get to see what "works" for you as a reader

- you get advice on how your paper looks to readers.

More people commenting on your paper = more chances to make it better. You might even consider seeking advice from a friend or roommate who isn't in your class. You don't have to follow all the advice you get from peers, because you know best what you want your paper to do, but you should consider it. One thing to note: writing instructors usually discourage peer feedback on grammar errors, especially early on, because we want you to focus on the ideas and overall vibe of the text (and also because not everyone gives good grammar advice, to be honest).

Writing Centre

Usually, your campus will have a place where you can go to get help with writing. Sometimes it's called the "writing centre"; other times, it may be called something like the "learning centre" or "learning commons" or some other name. Whatever it's called, you can expect the following:

- A one-on-one session with someone who is trained in responding to writing. Maybe a peer (a fellow undergraduate), or a graduate student who is studying something related to writing, or even a professional tutor who is more like a writing professor.

- General advice on how to improve your assignment in a "big picture" way – things like organization, expression of main ideas, and so on.

- Most likely, a reluctance to "fix" problems with your paper. Generally, writing centres see their mission as helping you to develop your own awareness and skills so you can improve your writing on your own.

A Paid Private Tutor or Editor

You may find that a private language-focused tutor or editor will be more willing to offer direct feedback on things like grammar, punctuation, and sentence structure. This can be helpful (and expensive!) but make sure you're not violating your university's academic-integrity policy: many schools will prohibit "unauthorized" editing. When in doubt, check with your instructor. I don't think professors should be scared of students seeking paid editorial help – after all, we do it too. (My writing is always much better when I pay an editor to help me check for errors, fix my citations, and so on before I submit something for publication!)

Grammarly, Spellcheck in Microsoft Word, or Other Software

These things can be helpful, but they can also be wrong, and can never replace a human reader. They can catch some big obvious mistakes, but because they're automatic, they overgeneralize rules in ways that often do not make sense and can easily "misinterpret" what you're trying to do in your sentences. (Really, they don't "interpret" at all, they just automatically apply rules.) A good program like this is better than nothing, but barely.

 TL;DR: It's always best to have someone other than yourself read something you write, and give you suggestions on how to improve it, before you turn it in. It's up to you whether to follow their advice, though. Software can help, but it's not perfect.

Vocabulary

Academic Words

I wish I could just give you a list of a thousand words and tell you that if you memorize them all, you'll be ready to read and understand anything. Sadly, it doesn't work that way.

Even if I could give you a list, it wouldn't be complete. Let's say that you know the word *concept,* which seems to appear in a lot of academic texts. (It means something like "a big, general idea.") Even if you felt comfortable with that word, you'd still have to make sure you know all other forms of it, like *conception, concepts, conceptual, conceptualization, conceptualize, conceptualized, conceptualizes, conceptualizing, and conceptually.* One word is now ten.

So instead of a list, I'll give you a few general principles, and some suggestions on where to look.

First, there are some general "academic words" – which really just means words that happen to appear more in texts that are used in universities and by scholars and researchers – that you should make sure you understand when you're reading. The best source I know for this is something called the Academic Word List, which was put together by Averil Coxhead from Victoria University of Wellington, in New Zealand. She did a *ton* of research, looking at millions and millions of words in academic texts, and created a list of the 570 most common words in academic English (not counting really common words that are used outside of academia as well, like *the* or *and* or *be* or *do*).

If you know these academic words, understand them when you read them, and use them correctly in your own writing, it will help a lot. I don't have a plan for how you should do this, but if you do an internet search for "academic word list," you'll get a lot of information and websites that have this list and ways to study it.

Second, depending on what you're studying, you'll find you have to learn *a more specialized vocabulary* – sometimes you hear people use the word *jargon* to describe this. For example, I studied English literature when I was an undergraduate, so I had to know what something called "iambic pentameter" was. (It's a kind of poetry that Shakespeare used. Don't worry, you don't have to know it.)

On the other hand, I didn't study economics, so while I know that "supply and demand" is something you hear economists talk about, I don't exactly know its technical, specific meaning within the field of economics. But you should, if that's your major.

Academic Phrases

In addition to specific words, there are also a lot of phrases that are commonly used in academic texts, and it's helpful to know them for both reading and your own writing.

Some researchers refer to these as "moves" that are commonly made in academic writing. The most famous example of this is what the researcher John Swales calls Creating a Research Space (CARS), something that writers of academic articles often do when they begin by establishing the importance of an area of research, argue that something is missing from that area, and explain how their own paper will fill that missing gap.

I can't list every single possible phrase, but in the case of CARS, here are some of the phrases writers might use:

The concepts of X and Y are central to ...

Very little is currently known about X in ...

Evidence suggests that X is among the most important factors for ...

One of the most significant current discussions in X is ...

I borrowed these from something called the Academic Phrasebank, which was compiled by John Morley at the

University of Manchester. I highly recommend its use – it lists hundreds and hundreds of common phrases, taken from real academic papers, organized by their purpose. Morley doesn't consider reusing the Academic Phrasebank phrases to be plagiarism, for the most part, and I think he's right. You can search for it online and even buy an entire PDF file of the phrasebook for under ten dollars.

 TL;DR: There are a lot of words and phrases that are more commonly used in academic writing than in other kinds of communication. The best way to learn them is to read a lot, and there are resources like the Academic World List and the Academic Phrasebank that can help.

Grammar

Grammar is the most important part of writing and language, but we can't really address it separately from any other part of language, because it's baked in. Everything is grammar. Diane Larsen-Freeman, a scholar who is probably one of the world's leading experts on teaching grammar, doesn't even call it "grammar"; she calls it "grammaring," to show that it's an active part of using language.

Most grammar resources are lists of things you shouldn't do. Personally, I have little to say about how to avoid grammar *errors,* because different people struggle with different things, and a lot of grammar advice is subjective. Rather than trying to "learn grammar," you'll do better if you practise writing, get feedback on where you might be making grammatical mistakes, and then learn more about how to fix those mistakes.

There are a few grammar things that I think you need to know, but keep in mind that everyone has different needs. Below, I have two pieces of advice based on issues I see in a lot of my own students' writing. It's totally subjective, but I believe strongly that I'm right and that everyone else's grammar advice is just folk tales and superstition. Here it is:

1 Ninety-five percent (or more) of the time *you can't join independent clauses* (basically sentences, things that have a noun and a verb that work together) *with commas* in English. You can do it in some other languages, but not this one. In formal written English, you have to use a conjunction, a semicolon, or a period.

NO It was snowing, we went outside.

OK It was snowing, and we went outside

OK It was snowing; we went outside.

OK It was snowing. We went outside.

OK It was snowing, so we went outside

OK It was snowing, but we went outside.

2 On a related note, you've got to be careful about where the punctuation goes when you use the word *however,* because if you're not, you might end up trying to join independent clauses with a comma again, which, like I said, you can't do in English.

NO It was snowing, however, we went outside.

NO It was snowing, however; we went outside.˙

NO It was snowing however, we went outside.

---

* Technically, this one could be OK if you had some stuff in the sentences before and after it that made the *however* function differently, like "It was very cold that day, and we had been planning to spend the day indoors. It was snowing, however; we went outside. No kid can resist the chance to play in the snow."

NO **It was snowing however; we went outside.**

OK **It was snowing; however, we went outside.**

OK **It was snowing. However, we went outside.**

That's it. Those are two things I think a lot of people get wrong and that you should pay attention to.

For everything else, I recommend that you:

- use a writing centre's website (e.g., Purdue University's Online Writing Lab)

- get a grammar textbook (see the "Further Reading" section)

- take a grammar class.

If you're really serious about understanding how grammar works, take a grammar or linguistics class in your university's English or Linguistics department. This might sound boring, but you'll learn a ton, especially if you grew up speaking English and never had to think about English grammar because it was already just in your head. I took grammar classes twice when I was a student, and I'd do it again if I had time.

 TL;DR: Grammar can't be separated from any other part of language. Lots of people use commas wrong, so learn the right way. Get a grammar reference book or take a grammar class if you can.

Sentences

Sentences are important, obviously. They don't have to be complicated. They should be clear and concise and relatively simple and not all that long.

The most important thing to know about them is that you should use a variety of types of sentences. To demonstrate this, I'm going to write three paragraphs below, each of which offers advice about sentences. See if you can figure out which one sounds the best.

Short sentences. It's OK to write short sentences. These are called "simple sentences." They're often short. They're pretty much just a subject and a verb. Sometimes they include other things. Another short kind of sentence is a "compound sentence." Those have a conjunction (like *and)* in them. You can write simple sentences and compound sentences, and they will both feel pretty simple.

Long sentences. Of course, if you use nothing but simple or compound sentences, your writing can begin to seem overly simplistic and dull, in which case you may want to consider the benefits of using more complicated types of sentences known as "complex sentences." These are sentences that have independent clauses (which usually just have subjects and verbs) but also have dependent clauses that can (for example) start with words like "which" or "that."

There are even "compound-complex sentences," which start stacking up all kinds of clauses in ways that can be somewhat tricky to follow, but which, if written well, can allow you to explore a number of different connected ideas while not losing your sense of "flow," though they can also start to feel unnecessarily long and complicated, especially if they happen again and again and again in a row.

Varied sentences. The point is: vary your sentence patterns. Simple sentences are too simple, and if you use a lot of them, your writing can seem brusque and choppy, as in paragraph no. 1 above. Compound-complex sentences, though useful when needed, can become needlessly long. You can end up confusing readers if you use them all the time, as in paragraph no. 2. Ideally, you'll use all different types of sentences. The first paragraph in this sequence felt too simple. The second one felt too complicated. This one is (I think) just right, and it's because of the variation in sentence patterns, which somehow feels more natural and readable.

 TL;DR: Use a variety of long (compound, complex, compound-complex) and short (simple) sentences throughout your paper.

Further Reading

Recommended Books on Academic Writing

There have been hundreds of writing textbooks written, but check these out. Any one of these books would be a helpful to read in addition to *TL;DR,* if your reaction to this book was TS;WM* and you want to go deeper.

Academic Writing: An Introduction, by Janet Giltrow, Richard Gooding, and Daniel Burgoyne

This has been the gold standard of Canadian writing text-books for some years for a reason. It does what *TL;DR* aims to do – that is, it's practical while still putting things in the larger social context academic writing happens in – but in a more eloquent and in-depth way.

Advance in Academic Writing: Integrating Research, Critical Thinking, Academic Reading and Writing, by Steve Marshall

This book combines some practical concerns about grammar and sentences with larger-scale stuff about how to write various versions of The Paper. The class on writing that I teach is based on this book.

---

* Too short; want more.

Mastering Academic Writing, by Boba Samuels and Jordana Garbati

I really appreciate the way this book takes students' experiences seriously and uses examples from students' perspectives. I think you'll find it very practical.

They Say / I Say: The Moves That Matter in Academic Writing, by Gerald Graff and Cathy Birkenstein

This short book is one of my favourites – it's clear and precise and gives you practical tips, including templates for how to write about arguments.

Writing from Sources, by Brenda Spatt

Most writing textbooks don't make the fact that you'll be mostly reading, summarizing, and interpreting other texts a focus, but this one does. It's quite long, so it's the opposite of *TL;DR,* but it's comprehensive and extremely useful. I highly recommend it.

Recommended Reference Books

A Student's Grammar of the English Language, by Sidney Greenbaum and Randolph Quirk

This book is out of print, but you can usually find it used on the internet for a good price. It's extremely detailed and can answer almost any grammar problem you might be facing, if you know where to look for it in the book.

Understanding English Grammar, by Martha J. Kolln, Loretta S. Gray, and Joseph Salvatore
This has been in use for a long time (I used the sixth edition in college twenty years ago). A helpful, readable, and practical grammar guide.

Publication Manual of the American Psychological Association
MLA Handbook
The Chicago Manual of Style
Make sure you get the most up-to-date versions – these change every few years.

Well-Known Books about Language and Writing You Might Not Want to Read

The Elements of Style, by William Strunk Jr. and E.B. White
Strunk and White are dead, so they can't argue with me, but there's no reason for this book to be as widely assigned in colleges and universities as it is. It's a collection of opinions about how language should be used, and it's interesting and useful as that, but it's not a manual for academic writing.

Fowler's Dictionary of Modern English Usage, edited by Jeremy Butterfield
Books like this are fun, but again, they have almost no relationship to the endeavour of writing well in the average

university course. (And again, Fowler died in 1933, which doesn't mean the book is bad, but I'm just saying.)

A Manual for Writers of Research Papers, Theses, and Dissertations: Chicago Style for Students and Researchers, by Kate L. Turabian
The author of this book is also not alive, so I may just be a coward. This book is actually really good, but only if you're certain you need to learn Chicago style, and not the more common MLA or APA styles.

Instructor Appendix
Activities for the Classroom

Below is a list of activities connected to several of the sections in each of the three main chapters of *TL;DR*. Some are adapted from assignments I learned about from my colleagues who teach in the Foundations of Academic Literacy program at Simon Fraser University; others are my own invention. You're welcome to use or adapt any that look like they might work for your classroom.

Chapter 1: Stuff You Should Know before You Start
Judging Sentences
The first activity I usually do in my writing class is hand out a sheet with seven or eight sentences on it, drawn from a variety of text types – nonfiction essays, novels, academic articles, business writing, scripture, whatever. I regularly update it with sentences that draw my attention. I don't teach a particular lesson on sentence construction along with it, although you easily could. Instead, I use it as a springboard to ask students questions like those listed below, which I think gets us all warmed up for more of

a metalinguistic or metadiscursive conversation. I'd rather the students start by explaining and maybe interrogating some of their own notions of what's good or bad about writing, because I hope they'll broaden their understanding of what that might mean throughout the course.

- Which of these sentences do you like or dislike? Why?

- Can you easily identify who or what is doing something in this sentence? (Why or why not?)

- What makes a good sentence?

- What makes writing good?

Identifying Audience, Genre, and Purpose

Another activity I use toward the beginning of my course is giving students four short excerpts of text with no identifying information. Often, I use a Wikipedia article, a film or music review, an email, and the introduction to an academic article. I have the students read the whole thing, and then I assign groups to focus on one of the texts and try to answer these questions:

- Who do you think the intended audience of this text is?

- What do you think the author's purpose or hoped-for outcome of the text is?

- What kind of text is this? If you had to give it a name, what would it be?

Sometimes they get it right away, sometimes they don't. I find that it helps here to really push each group to explain *why* they answered the way they did, using specific examples from the text. This is a good way to get people thinking about genre and genre features.

Musical Genre Features

Another genre-related warm-up activity I do is create a streaming audio playlist with a variety of songs from disparate genres. My current genre playlist is

- "Master of Puppets," by Metallica
- "Rhythm Is a Dancer," by SNAP!
- Beethoven's 5th Symphony
- "Can I Kick It?," by a Tribe Called Quest
- "40 Rods to the Hog's Head," by Tera Melos

This seems to be a good mix of familiar and unfamiliar songs for the students; even the songs they don't know have obvious genre features. What I like about this activity is that it's easy for some students to say things like "heavy metal," "dance," "classical," and "hip-hop," but everyone has to think a bit more when asked *why* we know how to label those songs with those genres. I try to explain that their familiarity with genre features has to do with their exposure to this music in its social context, and that they probably learned this from texts, media, friends and family members, or other symbolically mediated contact with the world.

We then talk about how this might map on to learning about genres of writing within academic contexts. It's also fun to find out how out of touch I am with contemporary music, though I try to blow their minds with that last song, which is "math rock," a genre that, according to Wikipedia, "is characterized by complex, atypical rhythmic structures (including irregular stopping and starting), counterpoint, odd time signatures, angular melodies, and extended, often dissonant, chords."

Analyzing "Content Course" Assignments

Depending on when students are taking your writing course, I've found a useful activity is bringing in an actual description of an assignment from another course and attempting to analyze "what the professor is looking for" – looking for words or phrases that might be unfamiliar to beginning university students and trying to "translate" them into concepts you might be using in a first-year writing class.

Chapter 2: Reading and Writing about Other Texts
Prereading and Reverse Outlining

Early in the course, I like to walk my students through a prereading or "reading around the text" activity by handing out a paper copy of an academic article. (I like to use the journal *English Today,* published by Cambridge, because it tends to run short articles with clearly demarcated headings, and I'm somewhat familiar with the subject matter, which is the English language as it is used, taught, and learned around the world. On a related note, I'm a fan of the "Writing about Writing" approach and feel that I can offer more to students if the things we discuss in the classroom are rooted in a discipline I know well.) I find the physicality of the thing helps everyone focus.

I send them on a kind of scavenger hunt to find the title of the article, the title of the journal, the publication date, the abstract, the reference list, and any other useful and common discrete parts of an article that may be present. I quickly define or ask the students to define each of these things as relevant.

Next, I break the article into sections and ask the students, in groups, to write reverse outlines of paragraphs in their assigned sections, using less than a sentence for each paragraph or group of paragraphs. Either verbally or on a whiteboard or a Google doc, we compile all the snippets of summaries into one big reverse outline of the whole text. This works well to help students see how these reading strategies can be used to break down the meaning of a text that might seem intimidating at first.

The Unreasonably Short Summary

I'm sure everyone assigns some version of a summary. One thing I like to do is start with unreasonably short summaries. Sometimes I'll show a one- or two-minute YouTube video – maybe a commercial or a political advertisement – and ask groups to answer the question, "What was that video about?" in a single sentence. We then discuss what some groups chose to include in their sentence and others didn't, and why. This is a chance to talk about some amorphous concepts like the "main point" of a text, and whether and how objectivity is possible in summaries.

Another short-summary activity I borrowed from my colleague Steve Marshall is the one-hundred-word summary. One hundred words is a lot less than it sounds, and asking students to summarize even something as short as a 1,000 to 1,500-word magazine article in one hundred words is a nearly impossible task, but I tell them to expect to be frustrated by this and to stick to the limit anyway. I have students read each other's short summaries in pairs or groups and look for two things in their partner's summary:

- any language reuse, no matter how long or short the passage reused (everything from single words to whole sentences)

- what things their partner included that they left out, and vice versa.

Both lead to fruitful discussions, whether on the nature of paraphrasing, quotation, and plagiarism, in the first case, or how we determine what is truly essential information and what is an "unnecessary detail" in a summary. (I later let them write longer summaries, don't worry.).

Believing and Doubting

This comes from Peter Elbow's classic *Writing without Teachers.* It's a simple exercise, but I find it a necessary counterbalance to the "critical = negative" mindset many students seem to have. There are a few ways to do what Elbow calls "playing the believing game" and "playing the doubting game," but I have two questions for students to ask about texts:

- What if everything in this text were true?

- What if everything in this text were false?

Sometimes I give them a short text about something ambiguous – for a few years, I used an article about the scientific study of near-death experiences, which was interesting because it touched on both highly subjective, nearly mystical qualitative accounts, of which many people are naturally skeptical, and the rigorous social science methods used for doing the actual research. I found students had to stretch a bit either way; I'd ask them to write a two-hundred-word response from the "believing" position or the "doubting" position. This gave them a chance to put some of the language of what I've called "stance" into practice, regardless of what they might actually believe.

Who Says What

This activity is meant to draw attention to attribution and can be done in a variety of ways. The simplest is to ask students to identify everything in a short academic article that is attributed to anyone but the original author of the text. This can be harder to do than it sounds: they may need to look closely at things that are not in direct quotes but are nonetheless attributed to another "voice." (This includes vague phrases like "some may argue ...")

I like to do an expanded version of this activity on a collaborative platform like Google Docs, in which the assignment is to identify every person or entity in a short article: any author cited, any text quoted or referred to, any organization or institution mentioned. The students can then make a list of these things and find relevant weblinks to them (e.g., a scholar's university website profile, a DOI for a journal article, or an organization's homepage). This sets up a future assignment about searching for sources, which I'll mention in the next chapter.

The Academic Integrity Spectrum

This is another activity I adapted from one of Steve Marshall's textbooks. I draw a line on the board and label one end "Totally OK" and the other "Punishable by death or expulsion." (I take some inspiration from my colleague Sean Zwagerman, who once referred to punishments of plagiarism as "the academic death penalty.")

I then provide a list of scenarios involving students getting "help" with writing assignments. My SFU colleague Andrew Flostrand's article "Undergraduate Student Perceptions of Academic Misconduct in the Business Classroom" includes a handy list of sixteen different scenarios, but you can create others based on your own experience.

In groups, students place each scenario somewhere along the continuum and then explain why they placed certain behaviours closer to the "good" or "bad" end of the spectrum. This allows us to have a nuanced discussion about plagiarism, academic-integrity policies, collaboration, and things relevant to the writing classroom like peer editing, paid proofreading, the role of tutors, and such.

Chapter 3: Writing "The Paper"

Everyone will have different ways of walking their students through The Paper, but here are a few things I like to do along the way.

Reading for Sources

This starts the same way as the "Who Says What" activity but expands on it. I ask students the following questions about a text, which they answer in a collaborative-text document:

- Who are the scholars and scholarly organizations mentioned in the text?

- What other texts are mentioned in the text?

- If it's a web text, what links are there to other texts?

- What else has the author written on this or similar subjects?

These questions will generate a jumble of people, organizations, and texts, which is usually just a disorganized list at this point. Next, I ask them to search for one or two articles written by the scholars mentioned in the text that are in the same general subject-matter neighbourhood.

At this point, I might ask them to start creating an APA-style reference list of potential sources to use for a short response or other type of paper related to whatever we're reading about. I might also have them generate a list of potential keywords to use to search academic databases for further relevant articles. The keyword list can take a while, and I try to have the groups learn by trial and error which words and phrases used in the original article seem to generate useful results and which are just idiosyncratic phrases the author happens to have used that won't help much when looking for additional sources.

By the end of this activity, each group has usually produced a list of five to ten solid articles that could be used as additional sources for a paper, and I allow anybody to use these sources if they want. (All the groups' lists are shared with the whole class.)

Bad Thesis Statements and Better Thesis Statements

This can be done as a stand-alone group activity or with actual thesis statements students have brainstormed for their own version of The Paper. Usually, we start with a dull, facile, or even obviously false thesis statement. Students then come up with two or three questions about the statement and then two or three counterarguments (this can also be done by trading statements in pairs or between two groups). The final product is meant to be a statement that has been inoculated by their own counter-arguments, or has become more sophisticated by anticipating possible questions readers might have about the position being taken in the statement. The activity might look something like this:

Original statement: **Airplanes are dangerous.**

Questions: **How dangerous are airplanes? What about cars, boats, etc.? Can anything be done to mitigate the dangers that do exist in air travel?**

Counterarguments: **There are many more auto accidents and deaths every year than airplane accidents and deaths. Airplanes are safer than they used to be. Crashes seem to rarely occur in some regions but more often in others.**

Better statement: **Despite the strides that have been made in air travel safety in the last century, certain steps need to be taken to lessen the risk of plane crashes in developing regions.**

The above example is certainly overly simplistic, and I probably wouldn't have my students write about airplane safety, but I find this exercise does help students think about how to make their thesis statements more nuanced.

Revision Plans

I sometimes ask students to write something called a "revision plan," which I first learned of from the website of the University of Michigan's Sweetland Center for Writing. My version includes just two parts, written in an informal list of bullet points:

- Briefly summarize the feedback you got from peers and the instructor along with any additional insights you have after rereading your draft.

- Write a plan that touches on specific areas you plan to change, how, and why, for your final draft.

My hope is that students' getting their thoughts together all in one place like this before they do a big rewrite will be helpful, but the key is to make it short and simple so it doesn't feel like extra busywork.

Acknowledgments

All of these people have taught me about writing at various points in the last twenty-five years; some in conversation, some in collaboration, some who edited or responded to my own writing, some without me having met them other than through their own writing:

Jane Thurlow, Mike Carrol, Christian Birrer, Brian Meier, TerryKay Birrer (*lux perpetua luceat ei*), Daniel Boatsman, Chris Chaney, Luke Reinsma, Tom Tryzna, Terry Santos, Suzanne Scott, Kathleen Doty, Nikola Hobbel, Corey Lewis, David Stacey, Andrew Shutes-David, Ling Shi, Ryuko Kubota, Patricia Duff, Anthony Paré, Sandra Zappa-Hollman, Steven Talmy, Steve Marshall, Susan Barber, Jan Maclean, Daniel Dunford, Ena Lee, Taylor Morphett, Janet Giltrow, Amanda Wallace, Kiyu Itoi, Greg Harder, Melek Ortabasi, Katja Thieme, Walter Ong, Kenneth Burke, Suresh Canagarajah, Paul Kei Matsuda, Peter Elbow, Charles Bazerman, Xiaoye You, John Edwards, Sibo Chen, Ian Kent, Saeed Nazari, Jiang Dong, Ismaeil Fazel, Tomoyo Okuda, Bong-gi Sohn, Rae Lin, Nasrin Kowkabi, Junghyun Hwag, Tim Anderson, Ching-Chiu Lin, Betsy Gilliland.

The "Flow" section uses material from the linguistics website Glottopedia under a Creative Commons licence.

Many thanks to Nina Conrad, Jennifer Walsh Marr, Julie Moore, Nadine Pedersen, Katrina Petrik, Lesley Erickson, and two anonymous readers for their feedback on this manuscript.

An enormous amount of gratitude to Sarah Heng Hartse for the hand-drawn diagrams (and for immeasurably more).

I'm grateful to the Collegeville Institute and the Lily Endowment for the time and space they provided for me to finish this book in the summer of 2022.

This book was written in many places in 2021 and 2022: on the traditional and unceded territories of the Coast Salish peoples; on the ahupua'a of Waikīkī, which has been home to Kānaka Maoli, the native people of Hawai'i, for many years; and on land that has been stewarded by the Ho-Chunk, Dakota, Ojibwe, and Anishinaabe peoples for generations.